T3-BIE-019

PUBLICATIONS OF THE UNIVERSITY OF PENNSYLVANIA

SERIES IN

Philology Literature and Archæology

VOL. IV.   No. 2.

SOCIAL CHANGES IN ENGLAND

IN THE

SIXTEENTH CENTURY

AS REFLECTED IN CONTEMPORARY LITERATURE

EDWARD P. CHEYNEY, A.M.

ASSISTANT PROFESSOR OF HISTORY

1895

AMS PRESS

NEW YORK

333.00942
C531N

Reprinted from the edition of 1895, Boston
First AMS EDITION published 1971
Manufactured in the United States of America

International Standard Book Number: 0-404-01523-9

Library of Congress Catalog Number: 76-168055

AMS PRESS INC.
NEW YORK, N.Y. 10003

TABLE OF CONTENTS.

CHAPTER I. — THE OLD RÉGIME.

CHAPTER II. — RURAL CHANGES.

SOCIAL CHANGES IN ENGLAND

IN THE SIXTEENTH CENTURY.

AS REFLECTED IN CONTEMPORARY LITERATURE.

———•◦•———

PART I. — RURAL CHANGES.

CHAPTER I.—THE OLD RÉGIME.

THE period which extended from the close of the fifteenth century through the whole of the sixteenth was a time of rapid change in many aspects of society. In the political and the intellectual world, in the domain of men's material and of their spiritual interests, there were new influences, new ideas, and new institutions. It was the transitional century from the Middle Ages to modern times. One of the most prominent characteristics of this period, and one which strikes us with a certain surprise, is the widespread and continued suffering of the great mass of the people. The contemporary literature, prose and poetry, sermons, pamphlets, private letters, court records, and statutes, reflect "the manifold complayntes of men, touchinge the decaie of this Commonwealthe and Realme of England, that we be now in, moved more at this present then of long time hathe bene had, some imputinge it to one thinge, and some to an other." [1]

We hear that "the state of England was never so miserable as it is at this present"; [2] and again, "England hath been

---

[1] *A Discourse of the Common Weal of this Realme of England*, p. 10. Lamond's ed., 1893. First printed 1581 and attributed to W. S., but recently shown to have been written in 1549, probably by John Hales.

[2] Thomas Becon, *Jewel of Joy*, *Becon's Works*, Parker Society ed., p. 435.

famous throughout all Christendome by the name of Merrie
England ; but covetous Inclosers have taken this joy and
mirth away ; so that it may be now called sighing or sorrowful
England." [1]

The most frequent complaints are from the country, but
town life also was troubled. The town craftsman in the
Dialogue says : " Therefore the citie which was heartofore
well inhabited and wealthie (as ye knowe everie one of youe),
is fallen for lacke of occupiers to great desolation and povertie." [2] In still another dialogue, the querist asks, " For who
can be so blynd or obstynate to deny the grete dekey, fautys,
and mysordurys here of our commynwele ; other when he
lokyth upon our cytes, castellys, and townys, of late days
ruynate and fallen downe, wyth such pore inhabytans dwellyng
therein ; or when he lokyth apon the ground, so rude and so
wast, wych, by dylygence of pepul, hath byn before tyme occu-
pyd and tyllyd, and might be yet agayn brought to some bettur
profyt and use ; or yet, above al, when he lokyth unto the
manerys of our pepul, and ordur of lyvvng, wych ys as ferre
dystant from gud and perfayt cyvylyte, as gud from yl, and
vyce from vertue and al honesty." [3]

Some of these complaints are no doubt merely instances of
the inveterate tendency of mankind to depreciate their own
times. When we are told

> " The worlde is changed from what it hathe beene,
> Not to the bettre but to the warsse farre : [4] "

[1] Francis Trigge, *Humble Petition of Two Sisters ; the church and the commonwealth ; for the restoring of their ancient commons and liberties which late Inclosure
with depopulation, uncharitably hath taken away.* London, 1604.

[2] W. S., *Discourse of the Common Weal,* p. 16, 1549.

[3] Thomas Starkey, *A Dialogue between Cardinal Pole and Thomas Lupset,
Lecturer in Rhetoric at Oxford,* 1536 (?). Early English Text Society, ed. 1878,
p. 70.

[4] Sir William Forrest, *Pleasaunt Poesye of Princelie Practise,* 1548 (?) Chap.
XIX, Stanza 27, Early English Text Society, ed. 1878.

we recognize a familiar enough statement in any time and in any country, and one which represents rather the temperament of the writer than the characteristics of his times. But much of the contemporary testimony is not to be thus accounted for. Men who were closely connected with real life spoke of the sufferings of real men. Sir Thomas More, before whom as judge just such matters were likely to come ; Hugh Latimer, who could compare the rent of his father's farm in his boyhood with that in his later life ; John Hales, who was the principal royal commissioner in an investigation of the inclosures in 1549 ; Robert Crowley, who printed and preached in the heart of London; the nameless composers of popular ballads and scurrilous pamphlets, — these and others rather as eyewitnesses spoke of what they had seen than as mere moralists bewailed the follies and the sufferings of mankind. Again, the changes that were in progress attracted the attention of the government, and a long series of statutes, ineffective, it is true, notwithstanding the authority of the Tudor monarchy, testify to the actual existence of those things of which the writers speak. Finally, the people gave the last proof that their injuries were real and their position intolerable, by rebellion. The very concreteness of the complaints, and the definiteness of the period in which they are heard distinguish them as real characteristics of the sixteenth century, not instances of the misfortunes which belong to all times.

A certain disintegration of mediaeval society had been in progress certainly since the time of the Black Death, but the particular group of changes which were now bearing so hardly on the people seems to have begun in the latter part of the fifteenth century, to have increased almost steadily during the first half of the sixteenth, and to have subsided only late in the reign of Elizabeth. There are a few isolated earlier records, such as that mentioned in the Parliament Rolls in a petition of 1414.

" And also they seiden that there was made great waste in
the same maner of Chesterton, of Housing, that is to say of
Halles and of Chambers, and of other houses of office, that
were necessary in the same Manor, and none housinge left
standing therein, but gif it were a shepcote or a Berne or a
Swynsty and a few houses beside to putte in bestes." [1] But
this probably represents the shadow of the previous century
of famine, pestilence and rebellion. The earliest undoubted
mention [2] of a rising tide of change in the position of the lower
classes of the country people is to be found in the speech of
the chancellor at the opening of the first parliament of Richard
III, in 1484, where he speaks of it as a matter of common
report that " thys body fallethe yn decaye, as we see dayly hyt
doothe by closures and enparkynge, by dryvynge a wey of
tenauntes and lattyng down of tenauntries." [3]

Somewhere between the years 1486 and 1504 a letter was
written to the president of Magdalen College, Oxford, " de-
syryng and praying yowe in god tenderly to remember the wel-
fare of owre cherch of Quynton, and the supportacion of oure
poer towne qwch fallys fast in decay and nere to the poynt of
destruccion except ye stand goud lord and turne more favorable to youre tenants, for youre howsynge gose downe, twenty
marke wyl nott sett up ayeyn that ys fallyn within thys four
yere." [4] Two statutes on the subject were passed in the reign

[1] *Rotuli Parliamentorum*, IV, 60 b., referring to Chesterton, near Cambridge.

[2] John Ross, a Warwickshire antiquary who died in 1491, in his *History of the
Kings of England*, gives a long list of villages already gone to decay in his time,
and speaks of his protest against the prevailing inclosures at the Parliament of
Coventry in 1459. But his work in the form we have it is only as edited by
Thomas Hearne, in 1745, and it is possible that the editor, who is not always
trustworthy, introduced some of these statements into Ross's manuscript. It is
almost incredible that the movement had gone so far so early in the fifteenth
century as Ross's testimony indicates.

[3] *Grants of Edward V*, p. lii. Camden Society ed., 1854.

[4] *Letter of Vicar of Quinton*, printed in Denton, England, in the fifteenth century, p. 318.

of Henry VII. Early in the reign of Henry VIII, More, reserving his universal irony for the second book, in the first book of the *Utopia* speaks plainly and definitely of the sufferings of the common people of England and their causes.[1] During the same years 1514–1518, the government was making another effort to solve the new problems. Somewhat later in the same reign appeared the ballad "Now-a-Dayes,"[2] and about 1536, Starkey's "Dialogue between Pole and Lupset," already quoted, while in 1533 and 1535, still a third group of statutes was passed on the same subject. In the later years of Henry VIII complaints became more numerous, as shown in the pamphlet and ballad literature, and in the scanty local records. But the greatest distress among the people, or at least the fullest testimony to it, falls in the short reign of Edward VI. Latimer and Lever, Becon and Gilpin, in their sermons, Crowley and Forrest in their doggerel verse, the Protector in proclamations and statutes, all dilate on the miseries of the people, and these finally reach their culmination in the rebellion of 1549. From the reign of Mary no mention of the difficulties has come down, except in the statute-book, where an act of 1553 adjudged as felons those "who to the number of twelve should break down hedges, ditches, or other inclosure of any park or ground inclosed," and another of 1555 reënacted all the old laws against inclosures, yet it is evident that the same causes were still at work, and in Elizabeth's reign they assert themselves frequently in the literature, as in Parliament. Midway in the reign, Harrison refers to "so notable an inconvenience growing by incroching and joining of house to house, and laieng land to land, whereby the inhabitants of manie places of our countrie are devoured and eaten up and their houses either altogither pulled downe or suffered to decaie by litle and litle."[3] A few

---

[1] See *infra*, p. 25.   [2] See *infra*, pp. 27, 36.
[3] Harrison, *Description of England*, Book II, Chap. XIII. New Shakspeare Society ed., VI, 1, p. 259.

years later, Stubbes declares that "these inclosures be the causes why rich men eat up poore men, as beasts doo eat grasse. These, I say, are the caterpillars and devouring locustes that massacre the poore, and eat up the whole realme to the destruction of the same. The Lord remove them."[1] At the very close of the century Bastard's vigorous epigrams give evidence at once of the improvement in poetry and the continuance of the social changes.

"To Queen Elizabeth.

I knowe where is a thiefe and long hath beene,
Which spoyleth every place where he resortes :
He steales away both subjectes from the Queene
And men from his owne country of all sortes.
Houses by three, and seven, and ten he raseth
To make the common gleabe his private land :
Our country cities cruel he defaceth,
The grasse grows greene where litle Troy did stand,
The forlorne father hanging downe his head,
His outcaste company drawne up and downe,
The pining labourer doth begge his bread,
The plowswayne seeks his dinner from the towne,
    O Prince, the wrong is thine, for understand,
    Many such robbries will undoe thy land."[2]

Even as late as 1604, in the first year of James I, a book already quoted sets out to prove of "Inclosure," that "(1) It decaieth Tillage, (2) It dispeopleth Townes, (3) It is against the Common-wealth of the Jews, (4) It is against the state of Christ's Church, (5) It is against Christian charitie, (6) It is against the Church and Commonwealth, and ancient liberties and customs of England, (7) Inclosure with depopulation is a

---

[1] Philip Stubbes, *Anatomie of Abuses*, 1583. Part I, Chap. VII. New Shakspeare Society ed., VI, 6, p. 117.

[2] Thomas Bastard, *Chrestoleros ; Seven Bookes of Epigrames*, 1598. Book III, Epigram 22.

sinne whereof God shall make especiall inquiry at the day of judgment." [1] But these last complaints are almost isolated. Notwithstanding the increased bulk of literary production, mention of the most characteristic of the changes is more and more seldom found. The period of the movements here referred to was evidently drawing to a close and giving place to a more settled condition of affairs for the masses of the people. That period was practically identical with the reign of the Tudor sovereigns, or can be said to fall pretty fairly into the century and a quarter between 1475 and 1600.

From much direct and indirect testimony, then, it is evident that some radical social changes were in progress during this period; that they bore with especial hardness on the lower classes of the people, and left a deep impress on the literature of the time. But in order to understand the nature of these changes, to appreciate the significance of much of the writing of the early sixteenth century, to see how and why so many people were suffering, it is necessary to gain some clear knowledge of the old English life by approaching it from the people's side, by recognizing its plain, everyday characteristics, before any great changes had occurred. For of all the group of contemporary changes, in the material, political, and intellectual world, there was none more profound than that in the ordinary life of the ordinary people. In fact, the problem we have to study in this essay is the effect on the masses of the people of the influences of this period: the period of the Renaissance and the Reformation, of the decay of the old nobility and the growth of absolute monarchy, of the increase of wealth and the extension of commerce, of the growing prosperity of the prosperous and the utter misery of the poor.

I. Mediaeval England was an agricultural country. It had of course its cities and towns, quite numerous, active, and wealthy, with their handicrafts and their commerce. These will come

[1] Francis Trigge, *Humble Petition*, etc.

under our examination later; but they were small at best, and the vast proportion of the people gained their support by agriculture and knew only rural life. This farming country of the Middle Ages, however, and its population differed in many ways, even as late as the fifteenth century, from that with which we are familiar in modern England.

The separate, isolated country house of the present time, whether gentleman's seat, farmhouse, or laborer's cottage, was almost unknown. The houses were all grouped into concentrated villages like those of the continent of Europe at the present day. A village street or open green was closely lined by the farmhouses, with their barns and outbuildings, of the whole surrounding stretch of agricultural country; and even the church, the parsonage, and the manor house were seldom far detached from the other buildings. Long afterward, the new habit of building houses separate from others was spoken of as an abnormal and perhaps somewhat impious thing.

"This community of dwelling, inclosers do sometimes take away in Christ's Church; for they will have no man almost dwell neare them. We may see many of their houses built alone, like ravens' nests, no birds building neere them." [1]

II. Outside of the group of houses of the village the country lay as open as in the "Angelus" of Millet. No hedges or fences divided the fields : the arable land, meadows, commons, and patches of woods stretched away uninclosed, and apparently undivided, till they reached the confines of another manor whose population was similarly gathered into a village surrounded by its open farming lands. From the farmhouses of the village men and women with their implements and cattle went out to work on their land, some of it perhaps a mile or more away, and returned to the village, on pathways which all converged, when their work was over.

[1] Francis Trigge, *Humble Petition*, 1604.

III. This open arable land was not divided up into farms in the modern sense, that is groups of fields, each field of some acres in extent, and each surrounded by a fence, hedge, or wall. On the contrary, the whole of the land surrounding a village was plowed into some hundreds or even thousands of "acres," an acre as a piece of land being approximately four rods wide and forty rods long. In some cases the division was into half acres, or even into roods, all these strips being of the same length, but of one half or one quarter the width, respectively, of a full acre. It is on an open field thus divided, that Piers Plowman says :

> " I have an half acre to erye [1] · bi the heighe way,
> Hadde I eried this half acre · and sowen it after,
> I wolde wende with you · and the way teche." [2]

These acre or half-acre strips were cultivated each for itself, and were separated from one another either by the mere reversal of the direction of the furrow in plowing, by narrow strips of unplowed turf, called "balks," or when the strips were on the side of a hill, by grassy banks known as "linches." The narrow balks or grassy strips separating the grain-covered acres were a conspicuous feature, and appear frequently in literature. They were the resting places where,

> " Between the acres of the rye,
> These pretty country folks would lye." [3]

Nicholas Breton makes his disconsolate lover say,

> " Upon some bushy balke
> Full faine I was to walke." [4]

And again,

> " Who can live in heart so glad,
> As the merrie country lad ?

[1] Plow.
[2] *Passus VI*, lines 4–6, Text B. Skeat's ed. Early English Text Society.
[3] Shakspeare, *As You Like It*, Act V, sc. 3.
[4] *Toyes of an Idle Head*, 1582, Chertsey Worthies Library.

> Who upon a faire greene balke
> May at pleasure sit and walk?"[1]

A man's farm was simply a certain number of these pieces of land, usually scattered in different parts of the arable land of the village.   He had no contiguous fields, but a piece here and a piece there, all over the manor, just as one finds the lands of the peasants scattered about in French or German villages to-day.   The Husbandman in the Dialogue says, "our grounde lieth in the common feilds, intermingled one with a nother,"[2] and the Doctor, "Every tenaunte had his landes, not all in one gobbet in everye feilde, but interlaced with his neighebours landes, so as heare should be three acres, and then his neighboure as manye; and over that, he other three or four; and so after the like rate be the most parte of the copie holdes that I doe knowe in this countrie."[3]   As the

---

[1] *The Passionate Shepheard, Pastor 3,* 1604. *Ibid.*
[2] W. S., *Discourse of the Common Weal,* 1549, Lamond's ed., p. 56.
[3] *Ibid.,* p. 124.

DESCRIPTION OF PLATE I.

Part of the open fields and scattered acres of the village of Nörtershausen, near Coblentz, Germany, photographed in the summer of 1894, showing (1) the concentration of farmhouses and barns in the village, (2) the absence of inclosures, (3) the cultivation in long, narrow strips in open "fields," and (4) the exclusion of cattle from the arable land.   More land, similar in appearance, belonging to the same village, lies beyond and to the right.   This arrangement is still characteristic of much of the agriculture of the Continent, as it formerly was of that of England.   Each farmer in this village has several of these pieces, in different parts of the field visible in the foreground, or in that beyond.   The woods to the left belong to the villagers in common.   The grain in the immediate foreground is growing on a strip in the open fields of the adjacent village of Oppenhausen.

PLATE I. VILLAGE AND OPEN FIELDS OF NORTERSHAUSEN, GERMANY; 1894.

PLATE II. VILLAGE AND OPEN FIELDS OF HAYFORD BRIDGE, OXFORDSHIRE, ENGLAND; 1606.

nature of the land usually allowed of quite a group of acres being plowed parallel with one another, access to his own acres was obtained by each man from a lane on which the strips abutted or at least from a headland common to all the acres in any one group or "furlong." But as the adjacent acres on both sides of his belonged to other men there was frequent opportunity for dispute. Gascoigne speaks of the plowmen who

> " set debate between their lords,
> By earing up the balks that part their bounds." [1]

And long before, Avarice had been made to confess,

> " And if ich gede to the plouh, · ich pynched on his half-acre,
> That a fot londe other a forwe · fecchen ich wolde,
> Of my neyhgeboris next · nymen of hus erthe.
> And yf y repe, over reche · other gaf hem rede that repen
> To sese to me with here sykel · that ich sew nevere." [2]

[1] *The Steel Glasse*, 1576. Arber Reprint, p. 78.
[2] *Piers Plowman, Passus VII*, lines 267–271, Text C. Skeat's ed. Early English Text Society.

DESCRIPTION OF PLATE II.

A plan of the manor of Hayford Bridge, Oxfordshire, England, before its inclosure. This survey was made in 1606, and is here photographed from a set of facsimile maps published by the University of Oxford in 1889. It shows the scattered acres, with the names of their holders and their measured areas, and the common pastures and meadows. The location of the village was in the northwestern corner. Lanes give access to most of the land. Certain inclosures are indicated near the eastern side, and what is apparently a cultivated knoll with linches is shown near the centre of the map. There seem to have been upward of a thousand divisions of land in the manor.

IV. The people were a nation of small farmers. Although there was a class of mere farm laborers, without land, they were comparatively few. Even the laborers commonly held one or two or more acres. At the other extreme, there certainly were large farms of a more modern English type, but these again were few. They represented usually the old demesne or home farm, which had been cultivated in former times by the lord of the manor and only recently rented out to a farmer on lease. There was consequently only one, or at most two or three such large farms in each manor or township. The typical farm of the fifteenth century consisted probably of some twenty or thirty or forty such scattered acres as have been described above. "For every fifty acres, forty acres, or thirty acres of land, one sufficient tenement mete for an honest man to dwell in," is the standard laid down in a later law.[1] Many of the holdings were still smaller. A government report of 1607 connects fifteen houses, each able to maintain a plow, with 250 acres of arable land.[2] Such a farm was worked almost entirely by the occupant and his family, but little hired labor being required, on the one hand, and the product being sufficient to support the farmer without his going out to service, on the other. The great proportion of the country population thus held, on one form of tenure or another, land which they cultivated as if it was their own. These "yeomen" or small farmers emerge into literary recognition just as their numbers were about to be depleted by the changes of the sixteenth century; but in one form or another they had long existed in England, and still survived to play a part in the events of the seventeenth and even the eighteenth century.

V. On every manor there was a considerable amount of land not divided into separate holdings but held more or less com-

[1] 27 Henry VIII, chap. 22.
[2] Ms. Petty Bag, *Depop. Ret.* Cunningham, II, 52, n.

pletely in common. Partly because population had never grown sufficiently to bring it into demand, partly because of its usefulness as pasture land, there was always an expanse which was not cultivated but allowed to grow up in rough grass and underbrush. On this extensive "common" the holders of the arable land had customary rights of pasturage, and opportunities of obtaining fagots, turf, gravel, or other requirements.

Moreover, in the mediaeval ignorance of any kinds of grass that would grow on dry uplands, the people were dependent on the natural meadows for making hay, and for purposes of pasture after the hay had been mown in midsummer. These meadows also lay open, though the portions which each tenant had a right to mow were probably marked. Finally, the pasture for cattle, horses, and sheep, in addition to that on the commons, and the stubble of the hay, was eked out by allowing them to feed on the portion of the arable land which was lying fallow or from which the crops had been removed. To make this feeding of the village cattle over the cultivated fields practicable, a compulsory rotation of crops existed, by which the holders of the strips in any one part of the open fields must all plant the same or a very similar crop so that it might be harvested from all the acres simultaneously, and thus leave the stubble and the grass on the balks available for feeding. Thus common rights in three forms, the "common," the meadows, and the plowed lands during their open period, played a large part in the agriculture and the social life of the group of village farmers.

VI. The holding of an ordinary small farmer, consisting of his house and its appurtenances in the village, his acres in the open fields, and his rights of pasture on the commons, was occupied by him on what was practically a fixed tenure. Some of the yeomen were actually freeholders; and however imperfect may have been the legal claim of others to the possession of the land, there was but little probability, during the Middle

Ages, of their being disturbed in its occupancy. In the stationary condition of population, tenants were in demand, and lords with superior rights over the land were but little likely to exercise those rights in dispossessing the occupants who gave to the land its only value to them. Therefore custom, so much more present to the common people than law, had made them used to secure possession and free bequest of their farms so long as they made the payments required in their leases or defined by immemorial usage.

VII. The close grouping of the houses, the system of open fields and scattered holdings, the common pasture, the small size of the farms, the permanence of tenure, must have combined to make the mediaeval manor to a great extent a single united body, separate from other organizations, but closely knit within. This union was strengthened by its usual ecclesiastical organization as a parish, and in the past had been still further embodied in the gathering of all the occupants of the manor periodically in the meetings of the manor court. This in its various forms of court-leet, court baron, and customary court, meeting at different intervals according to local custom, usually every three weeks, or in its more important meetings every six months, had brought together from time to time all the inhabitants of the manor. In these gatherings punishment of petty offenses, settlement of local disputes, interpretation and application of the "custom of the manor," drew the body of villagers constantly together, and perpetuated the fixed, invariable character of personal status and personal relations. It is probably true that before the middle of the fifteenth century the manor courts were in a quite general decadence, that meetings were not generally so regular, the sphere of activity not so large, and the attendance of the villagers not so universal. But even yet the local courts must in many cases have made a strong moral bond to hold the local community together, in addition to the economic bond of their agricultural system;

so that rural England might be looked upon as in a certain sense a league of some thousands of such manorial groups.

VIII. During the Middle Ages, absolute individual owner-ship of land scarcely existed either in conception or in reality. The older communal possession and feudal theory alike ob-scured the definiteness of land ownership in the modern sense. It is, therefore, not unnatural that in the fifteenth century the exact legal relation of many of the people to the land was somewhat ill-defined. And yet it was upon this legal relation that the fortunes of a great portion of the rural population were destined to depend. The manor (in the greater number of cases identical with the township of earlier and the parish of later parlance) was the unit of legal and territorial as it was of agri-cultural organization. It was the estate of a so-called lord of the manor. The king himself had always been lord of the manor in a vast number of cases, and many manors were still directly in the possession of the crown. A great number of manors belonged to ecclesiastical bodies, — abbeys, bishoprics, colleges, and chantries; others belonged to the nobility and gentry of all grades, from the duke or earl down to the lord of a single manor, who could seldom claim higher rank than the knighthood which belonged to all whose income from land rose to £20 a year. The direct possession of a considerable amount of land, known as the demesne, a superior claim to the remain-der, and many other rights on the manor belonged to the lord of the manor, whether this lord was the king, some great mon-astery, or baron with a hundred manors in possession, or the mere knight or esquire. In relation to the lord of the manor all its other occupants were tenants, that is to say persons holding from him.

There were four principal classes of the so-called tenants of the manor. The freeholders were practically owners of their land. Some vague feudal relation between them and the lord still existed, and there were certain payments in recognition of this supremacy, but otherwise they were free independent land-owners. They furnished a quite appreciable part of the yeomanry. Leaseholders — those who held their land on payment of rent, with a lease for a term of years, for life, or for a series of lives — were the direct tenants either of the lord of the manor or of some freeholder of land on the manor. These were "farmers," properly so called, those who paid a farm, ferm, or *firma* for the use of their land for a certain period.[1]

This class had had no existence in early times, but the economic development of the country had increased their numbers constantly. When the lords of manors had given up the cultivation of their demesne lands, these had been rented out as a whole or in parts to men who held them on lease, paying a money rent. Land escheating to the lord of the manor and land reclaimed from the woods or waste, when regranted, was usually treated as leasehold land. Some of this land was leased to large farmers and some of it was perhaps inclosed, but the greatest portion was in small farms of the type already described.

But the largest proportion of the rural population consisted of the customary tenants; those whose ancestors had held the same land from time immemorial, making customary payments in money or in kind at regular periods of the year, and on occasion of the sale or inheritance of their holdings. These were the villeins of earlier times, their personal services commuted for money payments, their serfdom for the most part canceled, forgotten, or simply disused because of its unsuita-

---

[1] Originally, of course, the word "farm" had no especial connection with agriculture, referring indiscriminately to anything let out for a fixed payment. In sixteenth-century use in England it is just obtaining its especial reference to agricultural land. "Upon his owne lands or upon his ferme landes" (Proclamation of Protector, 1549). "And though a man be but a farmer, and shall have his farm twenty years" (Fitzherbert, Husbandry, 1523), show successive steps in the restriction of its meaning.

bility to existing social organization, the tenure of their lands to all appearance securely fixed in long unquestioned custom, and in its comparative profitableness to their landlords. Combined with these descendants of the villeins of the earlier Middle Ages, must have been another element, a considerable number of small holders who had obtained the land they tilled otherwise than by long inheritance, but in the absence of a formal lease from the lord of the manor, ranking not as leaseholders but as tenants by custom. These customary holders were in many ways in an unusually enviable position for a peasant population. Laborious as was their life, numerous as were the burdens they had to bear, still the payments they had to make were based on a valuation made long before, and were now extremely light; they had all privileges of commons and common fields, and the lands they occupied descended to their children subject only to the customary fines. Those customary tenants, who had held their land from time immemorial, made up the class who were later generally known as copyholders. The rolls kept in the manor court consisted largely of records of the descent of such lands in something like the following form: " Richard Bullocke died, seised in fee of one customary tenement, called Moises, holden by the rodde at the lord's will; and that Richard is his son and heire, and seven years old, who by Robert Fabian and John Fabian is admitted tenant, and paies to the lord, for a fine, twenty pence." [1]

Below the customary tenants was a considerable population of laborers. Engaged for hire on the larger farms of freeholders, leaseholders, and even customary tenants, they were seldom perhaps without some land of their own also, if it were only a half-acre croft around their cottage, or a detached acre in the open fields; and without legal claims to the use of the common, they probably exercised such rights by sufferance.

[1] *Extract from Court Rolls of Manor of Coggeshall, Essex*, 2 Ed. IV, (1462). Dale, *Annals of Coggeshall*, p. 55.

In this description of the general organization of rural society in England about the middle of the fifteenth century,
there are two or three restrictions to be made.   The system
of concentrated villages and open fields was not universal.
As one approached the extreme western and northern portions
of England, those which long retained their Celtic population,
or those which had remained to late times heavily wooded, a
somewhat different distribution of population was usual.   As
Harrison says, "It is so, that our soile being divided into
champaine ground and woodland, the houses of the first lie
uniformelie builded in everie towne togither, with streets and
lanes; wheras in the woodland countries (except here and there
in great market townes) they stand scattered abroad, each one
dwelling in the midst of his owne occupieng." [1]   But the
organization described above was characteristic of by far the
greatest area, of all the more advanced, more populous, and
better known parts of England.   Again, a systematic description of customs and classes gives the impression of greater
uniformity and homogeneity than ever existed in real life in
the fifteenth or in any other century.   There were undoubtedly
houses detached from the villages, there were inclosures upon
the arable fields and the meadows, there were large farms of a
more modern type, there was competitive renting of land; yet
all these things were exceptional, not the rule.   Lastly, any
advantages and superiorities over the organization of society in
other times were relative, not absolute.   All mediaeval life was
laborious, subject to many vicissitudes, much privation, hardness, and brutality unknown to modern times.   But there were
also some advantages, and especially were there instances of a
better relative position of certain classes to others than had
existed in earlier times or has existed since.

With these reservations, the preceding description will indi-

[1] Harrison, *Description of England*, Book II, Chap. XIII.   New Shakspeare
Society ed., p. 259.

cate the framework in which the lives of the country people of England in the later Middle Ages were set.

This social organization was marked by three general characteristics: first, the large corporate or coöperative element in the life of the people; secondly, the close connection of the whole population with the soil; and thirdly, the extent to which the whole structure rested upon custom, not upon either established law or written contract. As regards the first point, it is to be noticed that notwithstanding the shocks to mediaeval society following on the Black Death and other occurrences of the fourteenth and early fifteenth centuries, the tendency to local organization and system characteristic of that period still remained. Men were primarily not individuals but members of a group. There was but little freedom of individual action. A man was shut in on every side, and at the same time supported on every side by the requirements of common action of his group. In the rural village life, the nature and course of the crops, the times of harvesting, the method of cultivation, the treatment of cattle, had to be the same for all the sharers in the open fields and common pastures. As already pointed out, the proximity of the houses of the village, its separation from other settlements, the local administration still preserved by the village group, the assembly in the manor court, the very shading off of one class into another, made this village community a corporation, a close, firmly knit body which has no exact equivalent in the more individualistic modern world.

Secondly, the connection and interest of practically the whole rural population with the land is manifest. There was a considerable number of small owners of land. There was a vast number of persons who occupied and tilled portions of the land by custom or on lease, as if it was their own. There were but very few persons, comparatively, who had no land at all in their occupancy. Small farms involve many farmers.[1] Therefore, whether a man was lord of the manor, a freeholder, a farmer on lease, a customary small tenant or copyholder, or perhaps even a day laborer, he had certain roods or acres which interested him as being practically his own; and he had still more unquestioned rights on land in the common possession of all.

Finally, this system was held in equilibrium largely by custom, not by law. The agricultural rules that defined the times when the fields and meadows were closed for crops and when they were open for pasture, were customary only. The management of common property, the powers of local officials, the distribution of public burdens between the lord of the manor and the tenants, depended on local custom. Not only everyday matters, as the burdens and the perquisites of the tenants, payments to be made, and conditions of tenure, but the rules of bequest, and the petty justice applied in the manor court, were defined by custom. That great body of wider national custom which had been frequently defined and applied by the royal courts, and had come to be known as the Common Law, settled a great deal, but there was also a great deal left by it to each locality to settle for itself. The "custom of the manor" was just as likely to be referred to as a determining principle, even in royal courts, as the doctrines of the common law. Yet custom, though it was for the time very strong, was necessarily somewhat indefinite. Moreover, if times should change and custom be strained, it would have neither the permanence nor the authority of common or statute law.

[1] The parish of Borley, in Essex, the figures of whose population happen to be forthcoming, in the fourteenth century had some 30 tenants who farmed their land, and only 10 who would rank as farm laborers. Of the latter all but 2 held some land in addition to their cottages. At present it has 3 farmers and 32 farm laborers, the latter either holding no land in addition to their cottages, or only a small fraction of an acre each. See Cunningham, *History of English Industry and Commerce*, vol. I, Appendix, for the mediaeval population ; also in a translation with notes in *Annals of the American Academy*, vol. IV, No. 2. The modern figures are from personal inquiry.

CHAPTER II. — RURAL CHANGES.

THE most important social changes of the fifteenth and six-teenth centuries consisted in the destruction or extensive modification of those characteristics of mediaeval society which have been indicated at the close of the preceding chapter. The passage from corporate support to much greater individual freedom, the separation of a vast number of the people from their close connection with the land, the substitution of contract and law for status and custom, — these made the real significance to a great part of the population of the passage from mediaeval to later society. And it was the incapacity of the great mass of the people to conform to conditions so rapidly and so fundamentally changing that made this time of transition so hard for the lower classes. Looking from the vantage-ground of long subsequent time we can now see what were the deep-lying influences producing change, reduce the varied phe-nomena of the time to some kind of unity, and judge of the ultimate results. But the men of that time saw only the details and the immediate processes; it is therefore from their refer-ences to these concrete changes that our insight into the char-acter of that time must be gained.

I. One of the great sources of complaint is the increase of sheep. Sir Thomas More, in 1516, complains that "your shepe that were wont to be so meke and tame and so smal eaters, now, as I heare saye, be become so great devowerers and so wylde, that they eate up, and swallow downe the very men themselves." [1] In a book already quoted, written in the

[1] *Utopia*, Ralph Robinson's translation, 1556. Arber Reprint, p. 40. The Latin original of this passage is as follows: " *Oves inquam vestrae quæ tam mites esse tamque exiguo solent ali nunc uti fertur tam edaces atque indomitae esse coepe-runt ut homines devorent ipsos.*" Original edition, Louvain, 1516; not paged.

year 1549, the husbandman says: "Yea, those shepe is the
cause of all these mischieves, for they have driven husbandrie
oute of the countrie, by the which was encreased, before, all
kynde of victual, and now altogether shepe, shepe." [1]   A tract
of the time, not dated, but evidently written somewhere between 1547 and 1553, is entitled "Certayne causes gathered
together, wherein is shewed the decaye of England, only by
the great multitude of shepe, to the utter decay of houshold
keping, etc." [2]   More than forty years afterward we still hear
the same cry of complaint about the sheep.

> "Sheepe have eate up our medows and our downes,
>   Our corne, our wood, whole villages and townes.
> Yea, they have eate up many wealthy men,
>   Besides widows and orphane childeren;
> Besides our statutes and our iron lawes,
>   Which they have swallowed down into their maws.
>   Till now I thought the proverbe did but jest,
>   Which said a black sheepe was a biting beast." [3]

Or again:

> "When the great Forests dwelling was so wide,
>   And careless wood grew fast by the fires side:
> Then dogs did want the shepherds field to keepe;
>   Now we want Foxes to consume our sheepe." [4]

Even foreigners noticed that near Oxford "such immense
numbers of sheep are bred on it round about that it is aston-
ishing," and near Cambridge "the countless numbers of
sheep." [5]

Sheep had, however, always been raised in England The
peculiarity of this time consisted not in the introduction, but

---

[1] W. S., *Discourse of the Common Weal*, Lamond's ed., p. 20.

[2] Published by Early English Text Society, in *Four Supplications*, 1871.

[3] Bastard, *Chrestoleros*, Book IV, Epigram 20.

[4] *Ibid.*, Book VII, Epigram 8.

[5] Jacob Rathgeb, *Narrative of Count Mümppelgart's Bathing Excursion to
England*, 1602. Quoted in New Shakspeare Society, VI, 1, p. lxxxi.

in the wide and rapid extension of sheep-farming. The earlier sheep-raising had been in the main simply a constituent part of ordinary mixed agriculture, and on most farms there had been scarcely more sheep raised than enough to provide the meat and the wool for local consumption. The great wool export which had been a source of national income and an object of royal taxation for centuries, was mainly the product of the demesne lands of monasteries or of other lords of manors situated in especially suitable parts of the country, increased by the occasional surplus of other farms. This, however, had made little or no impression on ordinary farming through the greater part of the country. A contemporary writer claims a divine authority for the earlier form of sheep-raising, which "convenyently occupied so much wool and felles, as the housbond-men and fermours in England receyved of the gift of Godd yerly by werk of housbondry in a right order, wher Godd first gaff the leyrs [1] thereof, when no singularte was sought to have more plenty of wolle by men's wisdome, than God by his wisdome first ordenyed, that alle men by ther bodily werke schuld receyve of Goddes gift bothe mete and clothyng togeders, that is with the werke of housbondry to receyve the speciall gift of the fynes and goodness of the staple wolle, which Godd by his first day of everlastyng light by vertu of his holy spirit gaff into the erth for the comon welth of Englande." [2]

But the sheep-raising which began to spread over England at the close of the fifteenth century was quite another thing. It was the substitution of sheep-raising for other forms of agriculture. This change seems to have been the result of three causes. The older agriculture on farms large enough to require hired labor was unremunerative. Wages had been higher for a

[1] Meadows.

[2] Clement Armstrong, *A treatise concerninge the Staple and the Commodities of this Realm*, about 1540. Printed in Pauli's *Drei volkswirthschaftliche Denkschriften aus der Zeit Heinrichs VIII. von England*, p. 15.

century, while there was no corresponding increase in the price of grain and other farm products.   The system of farming on open fields was cumbrous, slovenly, and uneconomical; and the soil tended constantly to lose its fertility.   Under such circumstances, whatever the degree of satisfaction of the yeomanry with existing conditions, employing farmers and landowners might be very willing to introduce a new system.   Secondly, there was a steady demand for English fine wool at good prices.[1] Not only was there the permanent foreign demand for its use in the looms of Flanders, France, and Italy, but also a new home demand, due to an extension of the manufacture of wool in England, which had been growing steadily during the fifteenth century, until it had become, as it long remained, England's principal manufacture.   The laborers required in attending to sheep were far fewer than in raising grain, and shepherds were paid less than any other class of country workmen.   Sheep-farming, therefore, was attractive in proportion to the difficulties of the older agriculture.   Lastly, capital unemployed and seeking investment was in existence in the towns, if not in the country, and could be applied, although with some difficulty, to farming processes.   The nature and effect of this last clause will be spoken of in another connection.   It is evident, however, that the introduction of sheep-raising on an extensive scale was a very natural step in agricultural development, held in check only by the usual intense conservatism of rural custom and sentiment.   And this conservatism might even yet have prevented any change,

[1] PRICES OF WOOL.

Date.	Per Tod. s.	d.	Date.	Per Tod. s.	d.	Date.	Per Tod. s.	d.
1461–70	4	11½	1501–10	4	5¾	1541–50	20	8
1471–80	5	4	1511–20	6	7¼	1551–60	15	8
1481–90	4	8½	1521–30	5	4¼	1561–70	16	0
1491–1500	6	0½	1531–40	6	8¾	1571–82	17	0

Rogers, *History of Agriculture and Prices*, IV, 305, 306.

if the old manor system had been intact, but slow changes had undermined its strength, its equilibrium was now easily destroyed, and sheep-farming was evidently spreading.

II. But sheep could not be raised in any large numbers in the open arable fields and common pastures which have been described in the previous pages. The sheep and cattle of the whole manor, in most farming districts, had been habitually pastured together under the charge of a village shepherd, cowherd, swineherd, or such official, or when they were fed separately it could only be in the narrow confines of the single acre or two, surrounded on all sides by the land of other men. If sheep in large numbers were to be introduced, considerable fields must in some way be inclosed, so that the owner could let them pasture at will, separately from those of other men, on a continuous stretch of ground, kept permanently in grass. Therefore three other processes followed immediately and necessarily : inclosures, the eviction of many of the previous holders of the small farms, and the substitution of pasture land for grain land. With these changes and some others which followed almost as closely, the whole literature of the time is ringing. It was here that sheep-raising became, for the time at least, a great social evil. It was these results of the introduction of sheep-farming which gave point to the oft-repeated figure of the sheep eating up men. 'To complete the quotation from the *Utopia* given above, the sheep not only swallow down men, "They consume destroye, and devoure whole fieldes, howses, and cities. For, looke in what partes of the realme doth growe the fynest, and, therfore dearest woll, there noble men, and gentlemen; yea and certeyn Abbottes, holy men no doubt, not contenting them selfes with the yearely revenues and profytes, that were wont to grow to theyr forefathers and predecessours of their landes, nor beyng content that they live in rest and pleasure nothinge profiting, yea much noyinge the weale publique :

leave no grounde for tillage, thei inclose al into pastüres : thei throw doune houses : they plucke downe townes, and leave nothing standynge, but only the churche to be made a shepe-house. And as thoughe you loste no small quantity of grounde by forestes, chases, laundes, and parkes, those good holy men turne all dwellinge places and all glebeland into desolation and wildernes. Therefor that on covetous and unsatiable cor-maraunte and very plage of his natyve contrey maye compasse aboute and inclose many thousand akers of grounde to gether within one pale or hedge, the husbandmen be thrust owte of their owne, or els either by coveyne and fraude, or by violent oppression they be put besydes it, or by wronges and injuries thei be so weried, that they be compelled to sell all : by one meanes therfore or by other, either by hooke or crooke they must needes departe awaye, poore, selye, wretched soules, men, women, husbands, wives, fatherlesse children, widowes, wofull mothers, with their yonge babes, and their whole houshold smal in substance, and muche in numbre, as husbandrye requireth manye handes. Awaye thei trudge, I say, out of their knowen and accustomed houses, fyndynge no place to reste in. All their housholde stuffe, whiche is very litle worthe, thoughe it myght well abide the sale : yet beeynge sodainely thrust oute, they be constrayned to sell it for a thing of nought. And when they have wandered abrode tyll that be spent, what can they then els doo but steale, and then justly pardy be hanged, or els go about a beggyng. And yet then also they be caste in prison as vagaboundes, because they go aboute and worke not : whom no man wyl set a worke, though thei never so willynygly profre themselves therto. For one Shephearde or Heardman is ynoughe to eate up that grounde with cattel, to the occupiyng wherof aboute husbandrye many handes were requisite." [1]

---

[1] Sir Thomas More, *Utopia*, Ralph Robinson's translation, Arber Reprint, pp. 41 and 42. The original is, " ut homines devorent ipsos, agros, domos, oppida

Shortly afterward, about 1520, apparently, appeared the ballad of "Now-a-Dayes."

> " Commons to close and kepe ;
> Poor folk for bred to cry and wepe ;
> Towns pulled down to pasture shepe:
> This ys the new gyse." [1]

And some twenty years afterward, in another longer ballad, it is declared :

> " Soe many shepe-maisteres
> That of errabell grounde make pasteres,
> Are they that be thes wasteres
> That wyll undoe this Lande.
>
> *　　*　　*　　*　　*　　*　　*
>
> And whye the powre men wepe
> For stowring of such shepe

vastent ac depopulent. Nempe abbates quibuscumque regni partibus nascit lana tenuior, atque ideo pretiosior ibi nobiles et generosi atque adeo abbates aliquot sancti viri non his contenti reditibus, fructibusque annuis quae majoribus suis solebant ex praediis crescere, nec habentur satis, quod otiose ac laute viventes nihil in publicum praesint nisi et obsuit, arvo nihil relinquunt omnia claudunt pascuis, demoliunt domos, diruunt oppida, templo dumtaxat stabulandis ovibus relicto et tamquam parum soli perderent apud vos ferarum saltus ac vivaria illi boni viri habitationes omnes et quicquid usquam est culti, vertunt in solitudinem. Ergo ut unus helluo inexplebilis ac dira pestis, continuatis agris, aliquot millia jugera uno circumdet septo, ejiciuntur coloni quidam suis, etiam aut circumscriptis fraude, aut vi oppressi exeunt, aut fatigati injuriis adiguntur ad venditionem. Neque quoquo pacto emigrant miseri, viri, mulieres ; mariti, uxores, orbi, viduae, parentes cum parvis liberis, et numerosa magis quam divite familia, ut multis opus habet manibus res rustica ; emigrant, inquam, e notis atque assuetis laribus, nec inveniunt quo se recipiant ; suppelectilem omnem haud magno vendibilem etiam si manere possint emptorem, quum extrudi necesse est, minimo venundant. Id quum brevi errando insumpserint, quid restat aliud denique quam uti furentur, et pendeant juste scilicet, aut vagentur atque mendicent. Quamquam tum quoque velut errones conjiciuntur in carcerem, quod otiose obambulent, quorum operam nemo est qui conducat, quum illi cupidissime offerant. Nam rusticae rei cui assueverunt, nihil est quod agatur, ubi nihil seritur. Siquidem unus opilio atque bubulcus sufficit ei terrae depascendae pecoribus, in cujus cultum ut sementi faciendae sufficeret, multae poscebantur manus." First three sentences from original Louvain ed., 1516; remainder, London, 1777.

[1] *Ballads from Manuscripts*, vol. I, p. 97, ll. 165–168, published by The Ballad Society.

> For that soo many kepe
> Suche number and such stawre
> And never was seene before." [1]

Inclosing, which is charged with so much evil in these quotations, meant the process of surrounding a portion of the common pasture or meadow, or a group of the acres on the open fields with a hawthorn hedge, so that the included portion might be retained for the separate use of its holder. This was inclosed or "several" as contrasted with its former condition of open, "champain," or uninclosed land. As Tusser says :

> " The champion differs from several much
> For want of partition, closure, and such." [2]

In a word, inclosures were fields, in the modern sense of the word, cut off from the old common pasture or open arable land by hedges. To many of us England can only have become England when its hawthorn hedges, white in May and green all the rest of the year, came into existence. Yet in Shakspeare's time hedges in much of the country must have been a novelty and still unusual, compared with their modern extent. Moreover, they were unpopular. Trigge says : " I have hearde of an old prophesie that horne and thorne shall make England forlorne. Inclosers verifie this by their sheape and hedges at this day." " May the cater pillars which God sent not many years since on thornes and hedges, which did eate off all the leaves of them in summer, may they not seeme to condemne Inclosers ?" [3] In the preceding century, the blocking of the old open ways by hedges around the new inclosures was referred to as a source of moral as well as material difficulty : " Tunc equites, viri et mulieres, praecipue senes et debiles anguriantur

---

[1] *Vox populi, vox Dei. Ibid.*, p. 125, ll. 65–68, and p. 126, ll. 81–85.

[2] Thomas Tusser, *Five Hundred Points of Good Husbandry*, 1557, p. 2, ed. of 1672.

[3] Francis Trigge, *Petition of Two Sisters*, 1604.

et coguntur ab equis et jumentis suis descendere pro portarum aperitione ubi antea nulla obsistentia solebant procedere. Pedites etiam et quandocumque equites alias vias per ambages et longiores vias artantas transire antequam veniant in oppositum viae inclusae et in dubium, non sine multis. maledictionibus pro talibus inclusoribus imprecatis.[1] The government report of 1517 mentions the hedges with the ditch which was usually dug inside: "Thomas Rowys armiger anno tredecimo Regis henrici septimi aput Clopton in comitatu praedicto cum sepibus et ffossis inclusit centum et viginti acras terre arrabilis de hereditate Johannis leighton armigeri et eas in pasturam convertit."[2] And an observant French traveler, in 1558, notices these among other differences from his own country : " Le pais est fort couvert et umbrageux ; car les terres sont toutes encloses de hayes, chesnes, et plusieurs autres sortes d'arbres, tellement que vous penses en cheminant que vous soyes en un perpétuel boys : mais vous trouveres forces escaliers qui sont appelés en Anglois amphores, et par là les gens de pied vont par des petits sentiers, et entrent dedans les terres.   Les gens de cheval n'y vont pas ; mais s'en vont par le grand chemin, entre arbres et buissons   En ce pays là, il n'y a point de bergers qui manient ordinairement les moutons ; mais on les laisse ordinairement dedans les boys, soir et matin, et dedans les prayries communes."[3] But the foreigner must have judged from a small section of the country, for in Leland we find about as frequently such entries as, "From Walton to Sherburne village, about an eight miles, by Champaine Ground, fruteful of Grass and Corne, but little or no Wood," as "the most part of the Ground betwixt enclosid."[4]

---

[1] John Ross, *History of the Kings of England.*

[2] *Inquisition of 1517*, ed. Leadam.   *Trans. Royal Hist. Soc.*, 1892, p. 182, n.

[3] Estienne Perlin, *Description des Royaulmes d'Angleterre et d'Ecosse*, 1558, p. 25.   Quoted in Introduction to Harrison's England, New Shakspeare Society, p. lxxxi.

[4] *Itinerary*, 1, fol. 66; and 3, fol. 74.

His description, indeed, would not have been true for any considerable part of England until the present century.

Sheep-raising, then, necessarily involved inclosing.   It is true that there were considerable difficulties in the way of inclosing land which had always lain open.   By statute law [1] the common pasture could not be so completely inclosed as to deprive the tenants of enough pasturage for their cattle or of easy access to their scattered strips.   According to almost universal custom, the arable fields must also be left open for pasture purposes during part of the year.   The great proportion of the small yeomen with their apparently well-established hold on the land opposed inclosures, and government soon threw itself into the breach and tried to put a stop to the whole movement.   Hedging and ditching was too expensive to be done for single acres, so groups of contiguous acres must in some way be constructed.   Yet, notwithstanding these difficulties, inclosures went steadily on.   The overcoming of the legal obstacles is too complicated and technical a subject to discuss here ; some of the means by which the practical difficulties were met will appear later.   The main point is to see how deeply inclosures, or the division of the open lands into modern fields, affected the country population.

Many of the inclosures were, as has been intimated, portions of the uncultivated common pasture.

"SUFFOLK [*Reads*]. — *Against the Duke of Suffolk, for enclosing the commons of Melford.*   How now, sir knave ?

2d PETITIONER. — Alas, sir, I am but a poor petitioner of our whole township." [2]

This may have had but little effect, except where the common pasture was so much lessened as to stint the villagers of their habitual opportunities for feeding their cattle.   But there

---

[1] Statute of Merton, 20 Henry III.
[2] Shakspeare, *Henry VI*, Pt. II, Act I, Sc. 3.

evidently were such cases. "They take in and inclose commons, moores, heaths, and other common pastures, wher-out the poor commonaltie were wont to have all their forrage and feeding for their cattell, and (which is more) corne for themselves to lyve uppon." [1]

"How join they lordship to lordship, manor to manor, farm to farm, land to land, pasture to pasture, house to house and house for a vantage. How do the rich men and specially such as be sheepmongers, oppress the king's liege people by devouring their common pastures with their sheep ; so that the poor people are not able to keep a cow for the comfort of them and of their poor family, but are like to starve and perish for hunger, if there be not provision made shortly ! What sheep-ground scapeth these caterpillars of the commonweal ? How swarm they with abundance of flocks of sheep !" [2]

This diminution of pasture land was a hardship for the villagers. But when the inclosures were on the arable fields another class of effects followed, which bore still more hardly on the tenants.

III. Occasionally one person, whether lord of the manor, freeholder, or other tenant, would chance to have several adjacent acres which could readily be inclosed in one field. But where the acres were all intermingled, as was more usual, the only practicable way to get the land into compact pieces for purposes of inclosure seems to have been to deprive the small tenants of their farming land. These yeomen without land, having lost their usual occupation, and finding no other at hand, had soon to give up their cottages, to wander in search of work up and down the country, as More describes them.[3]

---

[1] Philip Stubbes, *Anatomie of Abuses*, Chap. VII. New Shakspeare Society, VI, 6, p. 116.

[2] Thomas Becon, *Jewel of Joy*, pub. by Parker Society, in *Becon's Works, Catechism*, etc., p. 432. The spelling in the Parker Society Reprints is, unfortunately, modernized throughout.

[3] See above, p. 26.

Another writer about the middle of the century says, "And where that the sayde twelfscore persons were wont to have meate, drynke, rayment, and wages, payinge skot and lot to God and to our Kyng, now there is nothyng kept there, but onlye shepe. Now these twelfscore persons had nede to have living : — whether shal they go? into Northamptonshyre? and there is also the lyvinge of twelef score persons loste ; whether shal then they goo? foorth from shyre to shyre, and to be scathered thus abrode, within the Kynges Majestyes Realme, where it shall please Almighty God ; and for lacke of maisters, by compulsion dryven, some of them to begge, and some to steale." [1] In many cases the removal was immediate, from both house and land. It was this eviction of tenants, direct and indirect, that awakened the wrath of the moralists of the time, as it cannot fail to appeal to our own sympathy. The curse of the old Hebrew prophet was invoked again and again upon those who inclosed and depopulated their lands. "Wo be unto you therefore, that do joyne house unto house, and couple one field to another, so longe as there is any grounde to be had. Thinke you that you shal dwel upon the earth alone?" [2] "Wo be unto you which joyne one howse to another, and bryng one land so nye unto another, tyl ye can get no more ground, will ye dwell upon the erth alone?" [3]

"Again, how do many of the temporal worldlings join farm to farm, office to office, lordship to lordship, pasture to pasture, land to land, house to house, and house for avantage ! that the vengeance of God threatened by the prophets may come upon them : 'Wo be unto you, that join house to house, and couple land to land, so nigh one to another, that the poor man can

---

[1] *Certayne Causes Gathered Together*, etc., 1550–1553, published by Early English Text Society, *Four Supplications*, p. 98.

[2] Robert Crowley, *An Informacion and Peticion agaynst the oppressours of the pore Commons of this Realme*, published by Early English Text Society, p. 161.

[3] Henry Brinklow, *Complaynt of Roderyck Mors*, ab. 1559, published by Early English Text Society, p. 49.

get no more ground ! Shall ye dwell alone upon the face of the earth ? ' " [1]

When the old yeoman tenants, or the laborers, left their farmhouses or cottages, these were seldom reoccupied. The new sheep farms were larger and carried on by a higher class of farmers. As has been already noted, a stretch of country which had required perhaps one hundred and fifty persons to cultivate it in grain crops, when transformed into sheep farms could be looked after by less than a dozen. Therefore but few laborers could be supported ; and as a consequence many of the little villages became absolutely, many more partially deserted. The houses were merely a timber framework filled in with rough plaster and thatched with straw. When unoccupied the walls were dissolved by the storms, the roofs dropped in, and that decay which always sets its seal so promptly on a deserted house soon left nothing but obscure hillocks to show where many a little English hamlet had stood. Sometimes the unoccupied houses were deliberately pulled down. So the inclosers and evictors were spoken of as " pullers down of towns," "wasters of houses and villages," and "decayers of towns." The earliest law against inclosures, in 1489, says : " The Kynge our Sovereyne Lorde, havyng a singuler pleisure above all thynge to avoyde suche enormytees and myschevons, as ben hurtfull and prejudiciall to the comon wele of this his londe and his subgettes of the same, Remembreth that amonge all other thynges grete inconveniences dayly do encrease by desolacion and pullyng downe and wylfull wast of houses and townes wythin this hys Reame, and leyng to pasture londes whyche custumably have ben used on tylthe, wherby ydlenesse, grounde and begynnyng of all myschevons, dayly dooth encrease, For where in some townes too hundred persones were occupyed and lyved by their lawfull labours, now ben there occupyed ij

---

[1] Thomas Becon, *Preface to the Fortress of the Faithful*, ab. 1549, published by the Parker Society, *Catechism*, etc., p. 587.

or iij herdemen and the residue fall in ydlenes, the husbondrie whiche is one of the grettest comoditees of this Reame is gretly decayed, Chirches destroied, the servyce of God wythdrawen, the bodies there beried not prayed for, The Patrone and Curates wronged, the defense of this londe ayenst our enmyes outwarde febled and impeyred ; to the grete displeisure of God, to the subvercion of the policie and good rule of this londe, an remedy be not therfore hastyle purveyed."[1]   The next statute on the subject is named "An Acte Concernyng Pulling Downe of Townes."[2]   Just a century later, Francis Trigge speaks of "our cruell landlordes, our oppressors of their tenaunts, our pullers downe of townes, of whom as every age hath had some, so our age hath too manie."[3]   Indeed, this testimony to the decay of the villages is to be found everywhere.   "And further, yf you loke to the vyllagys of the countrey throughout thys lond, of them you schal fynd no smal nombur utturly dekeyd, and ther, wher as befor tyme hath byn nuryschyd much gud and Chrystyan pepul, now you schal fynd no thyng maynteynyd but wyld and brute bestys ; and ther, wher hath byn many housys and churchys, to the honoure of God, now you schal fynd no thyng but schypcotys and staballys, to the ruyne of man ; and thys ys not in one place or two, but gener-ally throughout thys reame."[4]   Hales makes his Husbandman say, "So that I have known of late a docen plowes with in lesse compasse then six myles aboute me laide doune with in theise seven yeares ; and wheare forty persons had theire lyvinges, nowe one man and his shepard hathe all."[5]   Or again, "For by your oppressors and extorcyoners, how be the townys and villagys decayed ?   Where as were eight, ten, twelve, yea,

[1] 4 Henry VII, chap. 19, 1489.

[2] 6 Henry VIII, chap. 5, 1514.

[3] *A Defense of These our Days*, 1589.

[4] Thomas Starkey, *Dialogue between Pole and Lupset*, published by Early English Text Society, in *England in Henry VIII's Time*, p. 72.

[5] W. S., *Discourse of the Common Weal*, p. 15.

sixteen howsoldys and more, is now but a shepe house and two or three shepardys." [1] Latimer cries, " For I ful certifye you, extorcioners, violent opressers, ingrossers of tenementes and landes, throughe whose covetousness villages decaye and fall downe, the kinges leige people for lacke of sustinaunce are famished and decayed." [2]

A contemporary of Latimer declares that " Satan, through Covetousness, doth so possess the hearts of many men, in these our days, that they do not only link house to house, but, when they have gotten many houses and tenements into their hands, yea, whole townships, they suffer the houses to fall into utter ruin and decay, so that by this means whole towns are become desolate, and like unto a wilderness, no man dwelling there, except it be the shepherd and his dog.

" Truth it is. For I myself know many towns and villages sore decayed ; so that whereas in times past there were in some town an hundred households, there remain not now thirty ; in some fifty, there are not now ten ; yea (which is more to be lamented), I know towns so wholly decayed, that there is neither stick nor stone standing as they use to say.

" Where many men had good livings, and maintained hospitality, able at all times to help the king in his wars, and to sustain other charges, able also to help their poor neighbours, and virtuously to bring up their children in godly letters and good sciences, now sheep and cowes devour altogether, no man inhabiting the aforesaid place. There beasts which were created of God for the nourishment of man do now devour man. The scripture saith that God made ' both sheep and oxen, with all the beasts of the field,' subject unto man, but now man is subject unto them. Where man was wont to bear rule, there they now bear rule. Where man was wont to have

---

[1] Henry Brinklow, *Complaynt of Roderyck Mors*, published by Early English Text Society, pp. 48 and 49.

[2] Hugh Latimer, *First Sermon before Edward VI*, Arber Reprint, p. 33.

his living, there they now only live.   Where man was wont to inhabit, there they now range and graze.

"And the cause of all this wretchedness and beggary in the commonweal are the greedy gentlemen, which are sheepmongers and graziers." [1]

We have not only general complaints like that just quoted, but the actual names, dates, and circumstances by which certain villages lost their population.   For instance, a last-century local historian with access to the manuscript records, gives the following plain unvarnished tale of the history of one little village, Stretton Baskerville, in Warwickshire:

"Thomas Twyford, having begun the depopulation thereof, in 4 Henry VII (1489), decaying four messuages and three cottages, whereunto 160 acres of errable land belonged, sold it to Henry Smith, Gentleman.   Which Henry following that example, in 9 Henry VII (1494), enclosed 640 acres of land more, whereby twelve messuages and four cottages fell to ruine, and 80 persons there inhabiting, being employed about tillage and husbandry, were constrained to depart thence and live miserably.   By means whereof, the church grew to such ruine, that it was of no other use than for the shelter of cattle, being with the churchyard wretchedly prophaned, to the evil example of others, as are the words of the Inquisition." [2]

The decay and the desecration of the churches and churchyards was an accompaniment of the depopulation of villages which was especially repulsive to the devout spirit of that age. It has already been more than once referred to in contemporary condemnations of inclosures and their results. [3]   It appears again in the ballad of "Nowe-a-dayes":

> "Envy waxith wonders strong,
>   The Riche doth the poore wrong;

[1] Thomas Becon, *Jewel of Joy*, published by Parker Society, *Catechism*, etc., p. 434.
[2] Dugdale, *Antiquities of Warwickshire*, 1765, p. 36.   [3] See pp. 26, 34.

> God of his mercy sufferith long
>   The devill his workes to worke.
> The townes go down, the land decayes;
> Off cornefeyldes, playne layes;
> Gret men makithe now a dayes
>   A shepecott in the church.
>
> The places that we Right holy call
> Ordeyned ffor christyan buriall,
> Off them to make an ox stall
>   Thes men be wonders wise." [1]

A later historian, in describing the country seat of Townley in Lancashire, calls attention to the fact that it had been formerly, apparently, the site of a village and chapel, "both of which must have been destroyed to make room for the house, offices, and grounds of the opulent family which followed. The small close now partly included in the kitchen garden is still remembered as the Chapel Lea, and it is said that human bones have been found there." [2]

IV. Sympathy with the sufferers by these evictions, and conservative dislike of innovation account for a great deal of the condemnation of sheep-farming and the resulting inclosures. But there were other more tangible evils asserted to follow, which attracted the attention of the government as well as of private men. These are well summed up in an address by John Hales in 1548: "Towns, villages, and parishes do daily decay in great numbers; houses of husbandry and poor mens habitations be utterly destroyed everywhere, and in no smal number; husbandry and tillage, which is the very paunch of the commonwealth, that is that that nourisheth the whole body of the realm, greatly abated; and finally the king's subjects wonderfully diminished; as these can wel declare that confer the new books of the musters with the old or with the

---

[1] *Ballads from Manuscript*, pub. Ballad Society, vol. I, p. 97, lines 153–164.

[2] Whitaker, *History of Whalley*, II, 186. A license for inclosing this place exists, dated 6 Henry VII, 1491.

chronicles." [1] There stands out here conspicuously the asser-
tion of two evils: the danger of loss from the cessation of grain-
farming and the supposed diminution of population.

"I condemn our covetous and new devised inclosures which
convert champion and fruitfull soiles, being good arable ground,
to pasture, casting halfe a cornefield to a sheepe's pasture.
And so thereby diminish God's people, and depopulate townes.
Secondly, I joine depopulation of towns and this new kind of
inclosure together; because the one of them doth follow the
other commonly, even as necessarily as the shadow doth the
body." [2] "Ther ys no man but he seth the grete enclosyng in
every parte of herabul [3] land; and where as was corne and fruteful tyllage, now nothyng ys but pasturys and playnys, by the
reson wherof many villagys and townys are in few days ruynate
and dekeyed." [4] Leland complains, "But always the most
part of enclosures be for pasturages." [5] The first statute of
Henry VIII on the subject is especially directed against this possible loss by the substitution of sheep-farming for tillage. "All
suche townes vyllages boroughis & hamletts tythyng housys
and other inhabitacions in ony parysshe or parisshis wythin this
reame, wherof the more parte the fyrst daye of thys present
parliament was or were usyd and occupyed to tyllage & hus-
bondrye by the owner & owners therof for theyr owne synguler
profytt avayle & lucre, wylfully be syth the seyd fyrst day or
hereafter schall be suffrid or causyd to fall downe & decaye
wherby the husbondry of the seyd townes . . . bene or hereafter shalbe decayed & torned from the sayd use & occupacyon
of husbondry and tyllage into pasture, shalbe by the seyd
owner or owners their heires successours or assignes or other

[1] John Hales, *Charge at Assembly for Execution of Commission on Enclosures*,
Strype, *Ecclesiastical Memorials*, II, ii, 352.

[2] Francis Trigge, *The Humble Petition of Two Sisters*, etc.

[3] Arable.

[4] Thomas Starkey, *Dialogue between Pole and Lupset*, pp. 96, 97.

[5] *Itinerary*, vol. V, fol. 84.

for them wythin j yere next after suche wylfull decaye reede-
fyed & made ageyn mete & convenyent for people to dwele
& inhabyte in the same, and to have use & therin to exercyse
husbondry & tyllage as att the seyd fyrst day of this present
parliament or sythen was there usyd occupyed & had, after
the maner & usage of the countrey where the seyd land
lyeth."[1] Somewhat vaguely recognized in this condemnation
was the fear that food would become more scarce, population
less, and the established order subverted. Moreover, the men
of the time felt instinctively that the passage from an arable
to a sheep-raising husbandry was a step backward. And they
were right; all history teaches that a society based upon agriculture is capable of a higher degree of civilization than is
possible for a pastoral society.

Whether there was an actual total diminution of population
may well be questioned, though it seems to have been the
almost unquestioned belief of the contemporary critics, at least
down to the middle of the sixteenth century. About 1536,
Starkey says, "Wherfor hyt ys not to be dowtyd, but that thys
dekey, both of cytes and townys, and also of vyllagys, in the
hole cuntrey, declaryth playnly a lake of pepul and skarsenes
of men. Besyd this, the dekey of craftys in cytes and townys
(wych we se manyfestly in every place) schowyth also, as me
semyth, a plain lake of pepul. Moreover, the ground wich
lyth in thys reame untyllyd and brought to no profyt nor use
of man, but lyth as barren, or to the nuryschyng of wyld
bestys, me thynkyth coud not ly long after such maner yf
ther were not lake of pepul and skarsenes of men."[2] And
again : "For thys ys no doute, in tyme past many mo have
byn nuryschyd therin, and the cuntrey hath byn more populos,
then hyt ys now. And thys ys les doute, that other cuntreys
in lyke space or les dothe susteyn much more pepul then

[1] *Dialogue between Pole and Lupset*, pp. 72, 73.
[2] *Ibid.*, p. 75.

dothe thys of ourys." [1] The summing up of the "sheep tract,"
referred to before, is as follows:

"Furthermore, as we do thinke, this Realme doeth decaye
by thys meanes: It is to understande and knowen, that there
is in England, townes and villages to the nomber of fifty thousand & upward, & for every towne and village, — take them
one with an other throughout all, — there is one plowe decayed
sens the fyrste yeare of the raigne of kynge Henry the Seventh.
And in som townes and vyllages all the hole towne decayed
sens that time; and yf there be for every towne and village
one plough decayed, sens the first yeare of the raygne of kyng
Henry the Seventh, then is there decayed fifty thousande
plowes and upwards.

"The whiche fifty thousande plowes, euerye ploughe were
able to mainteine vi. persons: that is to saye, the man, the
wyfe, and fower other in his house, lesse and more. Fifty
thousande plowes, six persons to euery plough, draweth to the
nomber of thre hundred thousand persons were wont to have
meate, drynke, and rayment, uprysing, and downe lying, paying
skot and lot to God, and to the Kyng. And now they have
nothyinge, but goeth about in England from dore to dore, and
axe theyr almose for Goddes sake. And because they will not
begge, some of them doeth steale, and then they be hanged,
and thus the Realme doeth decay, and by none other wayes
els, as we do thinke." [2] And Latimer's vigorous protest comes
to the same thing: "Furder more, if the kinges honour (as
sum men say) standeth in the great multitude of people. Then
these grasiers, inclosers, and rente rearers, are hinderers of the
kings honour. For where as have bene a greate many of
householders and inhabitauntes, ther is nowe but a shepherd
and his dogge." [3] Even in semi-official documents we find the

[1] 6 Henry VIII, chap. 5, 1514.

[2] *Certayne causes gathered together*, etc., about 1550, published by the Early
English Text Society, in *Four Supplications*, pp. 101, 102.

[3] *First Sermon before Edward VI*, 1549, Arber Reprint, p. 40.

same view taken : " Where there were in few years ten or twelve thousand people, there be now scarce four thousand ; where there were a thousand, now scarce three hundred, and in many places, where there were very many able to defend our country from landing of our enemies, now almost none. Sheep and cattle that were ordained to be eaten of men, hath eaten up the men." [1] Such a general depopulation was looked upon as a tangible danger. "And then, yf everie man should doe so (followinge the example of anie other), what should ensue therof but a mere solitude and utter dissolation to the whole Realme, furnished only with shepe and shepherdes instead of good men ; whearby it might be a pray to oure enymies that first would sett uppon it ; for then the shepe masters and theire shepheardes could make no resistaunce to the contrarie." [2] Sir Francis Bacon in his *History of King Henry VII*, speaking of the first statute against inclosures, says : "Another statute was made, of singular policy, for the population apparently, and, if it be thoroughly considered, for the soldiery and military forces of the realm. Inclosures at that time began to be more frequent, whereby arable land, which could not be manured without people and families, was turned into pasture which was easily rid by a few herdsmen ; and tenances for years, lives, and at will, whereupon much of the yeomanry lived, were turned into demesnes. This bred a decay of people." [3]

Yet notwithstanding this general testimony to a general depopulation, it is not at all certain that the total numbers were actually diminished. There was of course a considerable displacement of population ; certain parts of the country probably had more people in the early fifteenth century than they

[1] John Hales, *Charge to Commissioners on Enclosures*, 1549, Strype, *Ecclesiastical Memorials*, II, ii, 358, 359.

[2] W. S., *Discourse of the Common Weal*, 1549, p. 52.

[3] Bacon, *History of King Henry VII*, ed. London, 1819, vol. V, pp. 61, 62.

have ever had since. Nor is there any doubt as to the mass of disturbance of people, decay of towns, and consequent vagabondage and suffering. But on the other hand, nothing is more delusive than popular estimates of population at any time. Moreover, the inclosures and their resulting effects were by no means so extensive as we should infer had we no testimony other than the contemporary literature. Changes so fundamental, so complete a breach with the past, made an exaggerated impression on the minds of men, and they gave exaggerated testimony. A man who had seen a little hamlet which he had known to remain unchanged from his boyhood, almost suddenly reduced to solitude, its houses falling to decay, its open fields and pastures inclosed with hedges, sheep and cattle feeding in and out about the dismantled walls of its church and parsonage, and hearing in addition of similar troubles in other parts of the country, sprang naturally enough to the conclusion that the whole country was being immediately transformed. On the contrary, many parts of the country were almost untouched by the inclosures,[1] the statutes for the reintroduction of tillage were to some extent effective, and the process of inclosure was gradual, extending, even for that part of the country which was affected, over more than a century. Thus new opportunities for gaining a livelihood may have arisen during the same period, to lessen the severity of the shock, and to make possible a continuance of the same or an increased population. In the absence of statistical sources of information the changes of total population are not really discoverable, and the most that can be asserted is that the conditions were not favorable to a rapid growth of population, as they became later in the reign of Elizabeth. Nor does the other charge of

[1] See map in Ashley's *English Economic History*, vol. II, p. 304, and the sources from which the map is constructed in the previous references. But I am inclined to think this map somewhat fallacious, and the extent of the inclosures unduly minimized.

a diminution of the food supply seem to be substantiated. The price of grain did not rise disproportionately to other articles during the sixteenth century, except in certain years of known scarcity. This could hardly have failed to occur if there had been any serious decrease of production. It is probable that there were improvements in agriculture which caused an equal production of grain, although from a smaller area; doubtless some land was being restored to tillage even while new land was still being converted to pasture; and finally the stationary population made the problem of raising enough food for the nation a comparatively easy one. The importance of the rural changes of the fifteenth and sixteenth centuries lay in their influence on particular classes, on the relative positions of classes, and on the fundamental characteristics of social organization, not on the total numbers of the population nor on the total creation of wealth in the community.

V. One of the necessary results of inclosing the small groups of acres in the open fields and converting them into large sheep farms, was that there could be only a few large tenants where there were before many small ones. This resulted in a combination or consolidation of several small holdings into one larger one, and seemed like the willful dispossession of several tenants for the benefit of one. Such an "engrossing of farms" was a great grievance. "Furthermore in Englande sum one man kepeth in his handes two or three fermes, and where hath ben six or eight persons in every ferme he keepeth oonly a shepparde or wretched heardman and his wyfe."[1] A petition to Henry VIII, dated 1514, speaks of "unreasonable, covitous persones, whiche doth encroche daily many ffermes more than they can be able to occupye or maynteyne with tilth for corne, as hath been used in tymes past, forasmoche as divers of them, hath obteyned and encroched into their handes, ten, twelve, fourteen, or sixteen

[1] John Coke, *Debate of the Heraldes*, 1550.

fermes, in oon mannes hand attons, where in tymes past there
hath been in every fferme of them a good house kept, and in
some of them, three, four, five, or six ploughes kept, and daily
occupied, to the great comforte and relief of your subjectes of
your realme, pore and riche, for when every man was contented
with oon fferme, and occupied that well, than was plentie and
reasonable price of everything that belonged to mannes sustinaunce and relief, by reason of tillage," [1] and then proceeds to
ask "that no maner of persone from hensforth shall have or
kepe in his owne hands or possession any moo ffermes than
oon." [2]   Harrison says, "The ground of the parish is gotten
up into a few men's hands, yea sometimes into the tenure of
one, two, or three, whereby the rest are compelled, either to
be hired servants unto the other, or else to beg their bread in
miserie from doore to doore." [3]   In some verses of 1530, the
husbandman says,

> " But nowe their ambitious suttlete
> Maketh one fearme of two or three,
>   Ye, some tyme they bring six to one,
>   Which to gentillmen they let in farmage,
>   Or elles to ryche marchauntes for avauntage,
>   To the undoynge of husbandeman echone." [4]

And again, in a ballad of about the same date, the complainant,
after describing the destruction of farmhouses by the Abbeys
which were landlords, answers the question :

> " Howe have the abbeys their payment? "
>   " A newe waye they do invent
>   Lettynge a dosen farmes under one,

[1] *Petition to Henry VIII*, quoted in *Ballads from MSS.*, Ballad Society, vol. I,
p. 101.

[2] *Ibid.*, p. 102.

[3] Harrison, *Description of England*, Book II, Chap. XIII, New Shakspeare
Society ed., p. 260.

[4] *A Proper Dyaloge betwene a Gentillman and a Husbandman*, 1530, quoted
in Ballad Society, vol. I, p. 22.

> Which one or two ryche franklynges
> Occupyinge a dosen mens lyvinges
> Take all in their owne hondes a lone."[1]

Resulting from this combination of farms, was of course a scarcity of holdings to be rented. "And one man shal have two or three such thyngs or more, in his handys, that a pore man scarcely have an hole to put in hys head for these gret extorcyonars."[2] "For now the poore tenante that lyved well in that golden world ys taught to singe unto his lord a new song, and the Landlords have learned the text of the damned disciple, *Quid vultis mihi dare, et ego illum vobis tradam;* and nowe the world ys so altered with ye poore tenante that he standeth so in bodylie feare of his greedy neighbour — that two or three yeares eare his lease end, he must bowe to his Lorde for a newe lease, and must pinche yt out many yeares before to heape money together, so that in this age yt ys as easye for a poore tenante to marry two of his daughters to his neighboures sonnes, as to match himself to a good farme from his landlord."[3]

VI. Closely connected with the consolidation of farms was the rise of rents and fines. Rents, whether for lands on lease or for customary holdings, had been practically stationary from time immemorial. The same was true of the fines, or sums paid to the landlord upon obtaining or renewing a lease, or upon the acquisition of a customary holding. But now both fines and rents rose rapidly, and this increase, which seemed to be an arbitrary extortion by the landlords, was condemned most violently. It must in truth have been one of the severest hardships to the yeomanry who were the principal sufferers

---

[1] William Roy, *Rede me and be nott wrothe.*

[2] Henry Brinklow, *Complaynt of Roderyck Mors,* ab. 1542, Early English Text Society, p. 49.

[3] George Owen, *Description of Pembrokeshire,* published in Cymmrodion Record Series, vol. I.

under the changes of the time, and it was correspondingly blamed by their sympathizers. Latimer, in preaching before the courtiers of Edward VI, declared : "You landelordes, you rentreisers, I maye saye you steplordes, you unnaturall lordes, you have for your possessions yerely to much. For that here-before went for twenty or forty pound by yere (which is an honest porcion to be had *gratis* in one Loordeshyp, of a nother mannes sweat and laboure) now is it let for fifty or a hundred pound by yeare." [1] And shortly afterward he proceeds, in a frequently quoted passage, to compare the rent paid by his father for his holding with its present rate : "My father was a Yoman, and had no landes of his owne, only he had a farme of three or four pound by yere at the uttermost, and here upon he tilled so much as kepte halfe a dosen men. He had walke for a hundred shepe, and my mother mylked thirty kyne. He was able and did find the king a harnesse, wyth hym selfe, and hys horsse, whyle he came to ye place that he should receyve the kynges wages. I can remembre, yat I buckled hys harnes, when he went unto Blacke heeath felde. He kept me to schole, or elles I had not bene able to have preached before the kinges majestie nowe. He maryed my systers with five pounde or twenty nobles a pece, so that he broughte them up in godlines, and feare of God. He kept hospitalitie for his pore neighbours. And sum almess he gave to the poore, and all thys did he of the sayd farme. Wher he that now hath it, paieth sixteen pounde by yere or more, and is not able to do any thing for his Prynce, for himselfe, nor for his children, or geve a cup of drincke to the pore." [2] The cry about higher rents became louder and louder, and in fact continued after all the other changes which we are discussing had come to an end. "Con-syder you, what a wickednes is comonly used thorow the realme unponysshed, in the inordinate inhansyng of rentys,

---

[1] *First Sermon before King Edward VI*, Arber Reprint, pp. 38, 39.
[2] *Ibid.*, pp. 40, 41.

and takyng of unreasonable fynys, and every day worse than
other." [1]

> " A manne that had landes,
>   of tenne pounde by yere,
> Surveyed the same,
>   and lette it out deare ;
> So that of tenne pounde
>   he made well a score
> More poundes by the yere
>   than other dyd before." [2]

" So landlords make marchandise of their pore tenants,
racking their rents, raising their fines and incommes, and
setting them so straitely uppon the tenter hookes, as no man
can lyve on them." [3]

"The lande lordes for theyr partes, survey and make the
uttermost peny of al their groundes, bysydys the unreasonable
fynes and incomes, and he that wyll not or can not geve all
that they demaunde, shall not enter, be he never so honest, or
stande he in never so great neede. Yea, though he have ben
an honeste, true, faythfull and quiete tenant many yeres, yet
at the vacation of his copie or indentur he must paye welmoste
as muche as woulde purchayse so much grownde, or else voide
in hast, though he, his wyfe and chyldrene, shoulde perishe for
lacke of harbour. What a sea of mischifes hath flowed out of
thys more then Turkyshe tyranie ! What honeste householders
have ben made folowers of other not so honest men's tables !
What honeste matrones have ben brought to the needy rocke
and cardes ! What men-childrene of good hope in the liberall
sciences, and other honeste qualities (wherof this realme hath
great lacke), have ben compelled to fal, some to handycrafts,

---

[1] Henry Brinklow, *Complaynt of Roderyck Mors*, 1542, published by Early
English Text Society, p. 9.

[2] Robert Crowley, *Epigrams, Of Rente Raysers*, ll., 1369-1376, published by
Early English Text Society.

[3] Philip Stubbes, *Anatomy of Abuses*, 1583, New Shakspeare Society, p. 116.

and some to daye labour, to sustayne theyr parents decrepet
age and miserable povertie !   What frowarde and stoubourn
children have hereby shaken of the yoke of godly chastisement,
rennyng hedlonge into all kyndes of wickednes, and finaly
garnyshed galowe trees !   What modeste, chaste, and womanly
virgins have, for lacke of dourie, ben compelled, either to passe
over the days of theyr youth in ungrate servitude, or else to
marye to perpetual miserable povertie !   What immodeste and
wanton gyrles have hereby ben made sisters of the Banck (the
stumbling stock of all frayle youth) and finaly, moste miserable
creatures, lyeing and dieynge in the stretes ful of all plages
and penurie !   What universal destruction chaunceth to this
noble realme by this outragious and unsatiable desyr of the
surveiers of landes ! " [1]

The rise of fines and rents was treated universally as a delib-
erate and wicked exercise by the landlords of a cruel power
which they happened to possess.   Tyndale says, " Let Christian landlords be content with their rent and old customs; not
raising their rent or fines, and bringing up new customs to
oppress their tenants; neither letting two or three tenantries
unto one man.   Let them not take in their commons, neither
make parks nor pastures of whole parishes: for God gave the
earth to man to inhabit; and not unto sheep and wild deer." [2]

> " A pooreman whiche hathe bothe children and wief,
> Who (withe his parentes) uppon a poore cotte
> hathe theare manured [3] manye a mannys Lief,
> And trulye payed bothe rente, scotte, and lotte:
> A Covetous Lorde who Conscience hathe notte,
> by rent enhauncynge or for more large fyne,
> Suche wone to caste owte: it goethe oute of lyne." [4]

[1] Robert Crowley, *An Informacion and Peticion*, published by Early English
Text Society, pp. 165, 166.

[2] William Tyndale, *Doctrinal Treatises*, Parker Society, spelling modernized,
p. 201.   [3] Worked with his hands.

[4] William Forrest, *Pleasaunt Poesye of Princelie Practise*, about 1548.   Extract
in *England in Henry VIII's Time*, Early English Text Society, p. lxxxix.

A later writer with true old-fashioned readiness to settle the ultimate destiny of opponents, describes the soliloquy of the rent-raising landlords in hell. "Then, said Dives, wo woorth these racke rentes and unreasonable fines that shall purchase such a kingdome ! I would to God I might chaunge my estate of that kingdome with the most vilest and basest cottage on the earth. When they come hyther, they will crie out and say, wo woorth the time that ever we rackt our tenants, or tooke such fines to impoverishe them." [1]

Even the few advocates of inclosures were careful to explain that they did not approve of an arbitrary increase of rents. "But of one thyng, I pronounce and declare and take God to my recorde; that I make this boke onely to thentent that the lordes, the freeholders nor their heyres shuld nat be disheryt nor have their lands lost nor imbeselde nor encroched by one from another, and to non other entent. And for that I adver- tyse and exorte in Goddes behalfe all maner of persons as well lordes as other. That when the lord or freeholders knowe where their landes lye and what every pasture or parcell is worthe by the yere. That the lordes nor their owners thereof do not heyghten their rentes of their tenauntes or to cause them to pay more rent or a greter fyne than they have ben accustomed to do in tyme past. For as me seemeth a gretter charyte nor almes dede a man may not well do than upon his own tenauntes, for they dare not say nay nor yet complayne and therefore on their soules go it that so do and nat on myne." [2]

But one will hardly now believe that the landlords of that particular time were more selfish, reckless, and wicked than before or after, or more immoral than other classes were at

---

[1] Thomas Lupton, *A Dreame of the Devil and Dives*, 1584; quoted in New Shakspeare Society, VI, 6, p. 76.

[2] Sir Anthony Fitzherbert, *Book of Surveying and of Improvements*, Prologue, about 1523.

the time.   It is true that the twilight of the old faith and the early dawn of the new was a period of especial moral obtuseness, but it is hardly likely that the nature of landlords was transformed.   The fact that they raised their rents now while they had allowed them to remain constant for generations before must have arisen from an economic, not a moral cause. As a matter of fact, the rise of rents which fills so large a place in the complaints of the time, was in all probability a result of three quite natural concurrent influences.   In the first place, there was an increase of currency in the country, partly natural, through the products of the American silver and gold mines, partly artificial through the debasement of the coinage by Henry VIII and Edward VI.   This was claimed as the reason, even at that time, in the able *Discourse of the Common Weal*, lately identified as having been written in the year 1549.   The principal speaker, apparently representing Bishop Latimer, says: "And thus, to conclude, I thinke this alteration of the coyne to be the first originall cause that straungers first selles theire wares dearer to us; and that makes all fermors and tennauntes, that rerethe any commoditie, agayne to sell the same dearer; the dearthe therof makes the gentlemen to rayse theire rentes, and to take farmes into their handes for the better provision, and consequently to inclose more groundes." [1] And the same idea is applied to other prices, though not to rents, in another contemporary piece, of far lower dignity:

> "the cowne [2] it ys soo skantt
> that every man dothe wantt,
> and some thynke not soo skarese,
> but even as much to basse.
>
> *   *   *   *   *   *
>
> this coyne by alteracyon
> hathe brought this Desolacion." [8]

---

[1] Lamond's ed., p. 104.   [2] Coin.

[8] *Vox populi, vox Dei*, lines 412–15, and 434–5, Ballads in MSS., vol. I, p. 136.

The amount of silver in proportion to alloy in the standard coin was first reduced by Henry in the money issued from the mint in 1543; it was still further diminished in 1545, so that there were but six ounces of silver to six ounces of alloy; and again in 1546 to four ounces of silver to eight ounces of alloy, this last being still further debased by coining a pound, weight of the mixture into forty-eight shillings, instead of the old number of forty-five. Twice in the short reign of Edward VI debased coin was issued: in 1549 the silver being six ounces in twelve; in 1551, only three ounces in twelve, both issues being coined into seventy-two shillings to the pound in weight, the bullion value of the shilling of the last issue being only about one fifth of its nominal value. The proper fineness of the coin was not restored until the second year of Elizabeth's reign, 1560.

An influx of gold and silver from America began early in the sixteenth century, but only became of importance when the silver mines of Mexico and Peru began to be worked by the Spaniards, and even then only made its way from Spain into the west of Europe very gradually. In as far, however, as either of these causes existed, an increase of all prices, rent included, might be expected. But they cannot have been the sole cause; since, in the first place, a rise of rent is complained of before either of these existed;[1] and, in the second place, prices of many other things did not rise until long after the time of which we are speaking; as they should have done if the rise were due to the volume of currency.

Secondly, larger rents were asked for by landlords because there was greater production by tenants. A well-known chapter in Fitzherbert's Book of Surveying is entitled, "Howe to make a townshippe that is worthe twenty marke a yeare worth twenty

---

[1] Thomas Starkey, *Dialogue between Pole and Lupset*, about 1538. "And an other ther ys wych few men observe: wych ys the inhaunsyng of rentys of late days inducyd," p. 175.

pound a yeare "; that is, to increase its rental by one half,
and his receipt is simply inclosure.   However disadvantageous
sheep-farming may have been to those who clung to the old
methods, and even to the nation at large, to the individual who
practiced it it seems to have been immediately profitable.
From him the landlord could therefore exact more rent than
from his predecessor.   Inclosure and sheep-farming meant also
the addition of capital to agriculture, and persons who possessed this capital, or who were able to lease the farms
inclosed by the capital of the landlord, were willing to offer
him an increased rent, as they expected to reimburse themselves from the higher rate of profits obtained through this
investment of capital.

3· But, more than to any other influence, the increase was due
to the gradual substitution of competitive for customary rents.
In early times by far the greatest portion of the land had been
paid for by its tenants by a customary amount of labor.   The
money payments which were substituted for this labor have
the appearance of an ordinary money rent, but were evidently
defined in amount, not by the production of the soil, but by
the value of the labor they superseded.   As land came to be
granted out "on ferm," or simply for a money payment, this
also, there can be little doubt, was largely influenced by com-
parison with the amount paid by those whose rents came from
a customary or labor source.   Thus, until quite the close of
the Middle Ages the rate of rent shared in the customary char-
acter of so much of mediaeval life.   But now this was all rapidly
changing.   New methods were being introduced, new capital
invested, higher rent or a larger fine for entrance was being
offered by a new class of farmers.   "For, for to get your
neyghbours ferme, ye wyll offer and desire them [1] to take bribes,
fynes, and rentes more then they loke for, or then you your
selves be wel able to pay.   It is a wonderous thing to se gen-

---

[1] *I.e.*, the landlords.

tlemen take so great rentes, fynes, and ingressaunce for covetousness to advaunce theyr owne landes.   Howbeit it is a farre
more wonderfull thyng to see husbande men offer and geve so
greate fynes, rentes, incomes, yea and bribes for covetousnes
to gette other mennes fermes." [1]   It was natural enough, then,
that landowners should begin to look upon their land merely
as a source of income, to be valued at what it would bring.
The completion of the fate of the Rent Rayser, spoken of
above, is told as follows:

> " But when he was tolde
>   whan daunger it was
> To oppresse his tenauntes,
>   he sayed he did not passe.
>
> For thys thynge, he sayde,
>   full certayne he wyste
> That wyth hys owne he myghte
>   alwayes do as he lyste.
>
> But immediatlye, I trowe
>   thys oppressoure fyl sicke
> Of a voyce that he harde,
>   'geve accountes of thy baliwicke!'" [2]

Or, as Gilpin says, "As for turning poor men out of their
holds, they take it for no offence, but say their land is their
own." [3]   In fact, a new conception of the ownership of land was
rising by which it came to be looked upon, quite in contrast with
the feudal or communal notion of the Middle Ages, as subject
to the same completeness of control and use as any kind of
personal property.   This changing conception of land owner-

---

[1] Thomas Lever, *A Sermon Made in the Shroudes in Poules*, 1550.   Arber
Reprint, p. 37.

[2] See p. 47, Robert Crowley, *Epigrams*, 1550, lines 1377–1388.   Early English
Text Society ed., p. 47.

[3] Bernard Gilpin, *Fifth Sermon before Edward VI*, 1553.   Printed in *Strype's
Ecclesiastical Memorials*, II, ii, 134.

ship is indicated by the passage of the Statute of Wills, in 1540,[1] by which power was given to a landowner to dispose by will of all his lands held by a pecuniary tenure, and two thirds of his lands held by knight's service, a privilege which had been practically unknown for centuries in England. Thus it was again the breaking down of custom, not the especial wickedness of the landlords of that generation, that was the greatest cause of the rise of rents. Whether a man might do what he would with his own, was a question that had not called loudly for an answer during the Middle Ages, but now the landlords were answering it in their own way, and following up the answer, against the protests of tenants, preachers, and the government, by inclosures, evictions, and raising of rents to the highest terms that any man was willing to give. "And you surveighers of landes, that of 10£ land can make 20, you shall not be forgotten in the effucion of thys plage. For when you have multiplied your renttes to the higheste, so that ye have made all your tenantes your slaves, to labour, and toyle, and bringe to you all that may be plowen and digged out of youre groundes, then shal death sodaynly strike you, then shall God wythdrawe his comfortable grace from you, then shall your conscience prycke you, then shall you thynke with desparat Cain, that your sinne is greater then that it may be forgeven. For your owne conscience shall judge you worthye no mercye, because you have shewed no mercy."[2]

VII. Among the various complaints of the time one of the most common was of the intrusion of merchants and handicraftsmen into agriculture. A Petition to Henry VIII, in 1514, attributes much of the evil of the time to this cause. "Whiche misusages, and the inconveniences therof, hath not only be begon and rysen by divers gentilmen of the same your Realme,

---

[1] 32 Henry VIII, chap. 1.

[2] Robert Crowley, *An Informacion and Peticion agaynst the oppressours of the pore Commons of this Realme*, Early English Text Society ed., p. 162.

but also by diverse and manye Merchauntes adventurers, Cloth-makers, Goldsmythes, Bochers, Tannars, and other Artificers, and unreasonable Covitous persones, whiche doth encroche daily many ffermes more than they can be able to occupye or mayn-teigne with Tilth for Corne, as hath been used in tymes past." [1]

"Loke at the marchauntes of London, and ye shall se, when as by their honest vocation, and trade of marchandise god hath endowed them with great abundance of ryches, then can they not be content with the prosperous welth of that vocacion to satisfy theymselves, and to helpe other, but their riches must abrode in the countrey to bie fermes out of the handes of worshypfull gentlemen, honest yeomen, and pore laboring husbandes." [2]

> "If Marchauntes wold medle
> wyth marchaundice onely,
> And leave fermes to such men,
> as muste live thereby;
> Then were they moste worthy
> to be had in price,
> As men that provide us
> of all kyndes marchaundice.
> But syth they take fermes,
> to let them out agayne,
> To such men as muste have them,
> though it be to theyr payn:
> And to leavye greate fines,
> or to over the rent,
> And do purchayse greate landes
> for the same intent:
> We must nedes cal them
> membres unprofitable
> As men that woulde make
> All the Realme miserable." [8]

---

[1] Printed in Ballad Society Publications, vol. I, p. 101.

[2] Thomas Lever, *A Sermon made in the Shroudes in Poules*, 1550, Arber Reprint, p. 29.

[8] Robert Crowley, *Epigrams*, lines 1193–1210.

The feeling of the time was very clearly that each class should keep to its own occupation.

> " The landlord with his terme,
>   the plowght man with his ferme,
>   the kneght wyth his fare,
>   the marchant with his ware.
>   then showld increse the helth
>   of yche comon welthe." [1]

Even when the larger landlords took their farms into their own hands, and themselves entered the ranks of cultivators it was looked upon as a great evil, though it was but reverting to a custom of earlier times, when it had indeed been of great general advantage. Still, the feeling was that " it was never merie with poore craftes men since gentlemen became grasiers." [2] The knight defends his class by saying : " And suche of us as doe abyde in the countrie still can not with 200£ a yeare kepe that house, that we might have done with 200 marks but sixteen yeares agoe. And therfore we are forced either to minyshe the third parte of our houshold, or to raise the thirde part of oure Revenues. And for that we can not so doe of our landes, that is alreadie in the hands of other men, many of us are forced either to kepe parte of their owne landes when they fall into theire owne possessions, or to purchase some ferme of other mens landes, and to store it with shepe or some other catall to helpe to make up the decaye of their revenues and to maintaine theire old estate with all." [3] But for city merchants to come out into the country and buy up lands, either to rent out again or to occupy themselves as cultivators, seemed absolutely indefensible.

> " So sone as they have oughte to spare,
>   Besyde theyr stocke that muste remayne,

---

[1] *Vox populi, vox Dei*, lines 337–342, Ballad Society Publications, vol. I, p. 133.

[2] W. S., *Discourse of the Common Weal*, 1549, p. 18.

[3] *Ibid.*, p. 20.

To purchase landes is al theyre care
And all the study of theyre brayne,
    Ther can be none unthrifty heyre,
Whome they will not smel out anon,
And handle him with wordes ful fayre,
Tel al his landes is from him gone.
    The fermes, the woodes, and pasture grounds,
That do lye round about London,
Are hedged in within their mowndes,
Or else shalbe ere they have done.
    They have their spies upon eche syde
To se when ought is lyke to fal;
And as sone as ought can be spied,
They are ready at the fyrst cal.

*   *   *   *   *   *   *

    For in the worlde ther can not be
More greate abhomination,
To thy Lorde God, then is in the
Forsakeyng thy vocation." [1]

" Merchaunt men travell the contre
    plowmen Dwell in the cyte,
Which wyll Destroy the land shortly:
    That will be sene in hast!" [2]

" For the statte of all youre marchant men
undo most parte of youre gentyll men,
and wrape them in suche bandes
that they have halle their lands." [3]

" Therefore the devyll poysonynge all hys wyth greadye
covetousness, wyll cause them ever to trust to their owne
provision, and never to be content wyth their owne vocacion,
but beynge called of God to be marchaunt, gentleman, lawyer,
or courtear yet to be readye at a becke of their father the
devyl, besydes this their godly vocation devyllyshelye to proule

[1] Robert Crowley, *The Last Trumpet, The Marchauntes Lesson*, lines 1065–
1080, and 1173–1176.
[2] Ballad, *Nowe-a-Dayes*, 1520, lines 181–184, Ballad Society Publications, I,
p. 87.
[3] Ballad, *Vox populi, vox Dei*, lines 267–270.

for, seke, and purchase farmes, personages, and benefices, to discourage housbandemenne from tyllynge of the grounde and ministers from preachynge of Godde's woorde." [1]

This invasion of the country by the town merchants is readily explicable. Such capital as existed in England was largely the product of city trade and commerce and city handicrafts. Manufactures and foreign trade had both been increasing in England through the whole of the fifteenth century. Much wealth had thus been accumulated in the towns. In the country, on the contrary, there had been but little surplus of wealth created. The agriculture was, as has been seen, mainly for the self-support of the farmers, not for profit. The income of the gentry had in the past been largely wasted in the Wars of the Roses, and was now being absorbed in those growing habits of expenditure when men

> " Broke their backs with laying manors on them." [2]

The town was relatively rich, the country was poor. But opportunities for investment of capital in the towns were not sufficient, so when the agricultural changes indicated by inclosing and sheep-raising showed themselves in the country, it was natural enough that merchants and well-to-do burghers of all occupations should buy up these lands as an investment, or take up large farming as an occupation. Moreover, it is very probable that many of the townsmen were themselves only separated from the country families by a few generations. There are evidences of a migration of younger sons or broken members of the old country gentry to the towns for long periods before, and it may be that now, in many cases, they were only as a class repurchasing the lands which the more impoverished older branches were no longer able to keep. Harrison says, in speaking of merchants, "they often change

[1] Thomas Lever, *A Sermon made in the Shroudes in Poules*, 1550, Arber Reprint, p. 50.
[2] Shakspeare, *Henry VIII*, Act I, Sc. 1.

estate with gentlemen, as gentlemen doo with them, by a mutuall conversion of the one into the other." [1] The exchange of population and of capital between country and city has been an oft-repeated phenomenon from ancient to present times. During the late fifteenth and the sixteenth century the movement seems to have been from the town to the rural districts. " Every gentylman flyth into the countrey. Few that inhabyt cytes or townys, few that have any regard of them." [2]

There was, however, an especial accompaniment of this transfer of capital which must have been frequently injurious, as it was certainly extremely obnoxious to men of that time. A class of men seems to have made a business of buying up leases, or the right to rent the land for a given number of years, not becoming themselves actual owners of the land nor intending to be its occupants. They wanted the leases for the purpose of speculation ; that is, to let the farms out again at an advanced rate, making their own profit by the difference between what they had paid to the landlord and what they could extract from the tenant. " On the other syde, ther bee certayne tenauntes, not able to be landelordes, and yet, after a sorte, they counterfayte landelordes, by obtaynyge leases in and upon grounde and tenementes, and so reyse fynes, incomes, and rentes ; and by suche pyllage pyke out a porcion to mayntayne a proude porte, and all by pylynge and pollynge of the poore commons, that must of necessitie seke habitations at their handes." [3] " And doubte ye not, you lease mongers, that take groundes by lease to the entente to lette them out agayne for double and tryple the rent, your part is in this plage." [4]

[1] *Description of England*, Book II, chap. V, New Shakspeare Society, VII, I, p. 131.

[2] Thomas Starkey, *Dialogue between Pole and Lupset*, Early English Text Society ed., p. 93.

[3] Robert Crowley, *An Informacion and Peticion*, Early English Text Society ed., pp. 166, 167.   [4] *Ibid.*, p. 162.

These middlemen and "lease-mongers" were the object of unsparing denunciation.

> " Reversions of fermes
> are bought on ech syde ;
> And the olde tenant must pay well,
> if he wyll a byde.
> And where the father payde a peny,
> and a capon or twayne,
> The sonne muste paye ten pounde.
> This passeth my brayne.
> Well, let thes forestallars
> repent them bytyme,
> Leste the clarke of the market
> be wyth them ere pryme.
> For he, when he cometh,
> wyll punysh them all,
> That do any nedeful thynge
> ingrose or forestall." [1]

" There is a lyke maner of barganyng of them that be lease-mongers, for leasemongers make the tenaunts to pay so muche, and the landlord to take so little, that neither of them is wel able to kepe house. I heare say that within a few miles of London an honest gentlemen did let his ground by lease unto pore honest men after 2s. 4d. an acar : then commeth a lese-mounger, a thefe, an extorcioner, deceivyng ye tenaunts, bieth theyr leases, put theim from the groundes, and causeth them yat have it at hym nowe, to paye after 9s., or as I harde saye, 19s., but I am ashamed to name so muche.   How be it, covetous extorcioners be ashamed of no dede be it never so evyll." [2] "Forestalling," buying up goods before other buyers had a chance to join in their purchase, had always been condemned, and had indeed been quite effectually prevented for most com-

[1] Robert Crowley, *Epigrams, Of Forestallers*, lines 957–972, Early English Text Society ed., p. 34.

[2] Thomas Lever, *A Sermon preached at Paule's Crosse*, 1530, Arber Reprint, p. 129.

modities by gild ordinances or other local regulations, or by statute law. But buying of leases was forestalling of the most necessary of all commodities, land. In order to realize the effect of such a practice, one must picture the ignorant and somewhat stolid tenants of small farms in the country, or of little houses in the towns, relying entirely on old custom, and on a code of morals and law, which consisted largely in conforming to this established custom. These people now found themselves confronted with a man shrewd, business-like, possessed of capital, and clothed with a recently acquired legal right to turn them out of their holdings, or, if he preferred, to require a large fine from the tenants for permission to retain their holdings, and afterward demand a much greater rent than had been customarily paid. Of course parallels are to be found in modern India, Russia, Ireland, or perhaps even nearer home, but it is no wonder that with the but slightly developed belief in the rightfulness of pure competition existing in the sixteenth century, men like Latimer or Crowley should say,

> " Lord God ! (quod this marchaunt)
>   in Turkye have I bene,
> Yet emonge those heathen
>   none such crueltie have I sene." [1]

Or that they should picture their final destination with such clearness of vision.

> " Of late a leasemongar
>   of London laye sycke,
> And thynckyng to dye
>   his conscience dyd him pricke.
> Wherefore he sayde thus
>   wyth hym selfe secretly,
> ' I wyll sende for a preachar,
>   to knowe what remedy.'

---

[1] Robert Crowley, *Epigrams*, lines 237–240.

But whilse he thus laye,
   he fell in a sloumber,
And sawe in his dreame
   pore folke a greate number.
Whoe sayde they had learned thys
   at the preachars hande,
To paye all wyth patience,
   that theyr landlordes demaunde.
For they for theyr sufferaunce,
   in such oppression,
Are promised rewarde
   in the resurrection.
Where such men as take leases
   them selves to advaunce,
Are sure to have hell
   by ryght inheritaunce." [1]

VIII. The dissolution of the monasteries between 1536 and 1540 was recognized at the time as having an important bearing on the prevalent agricultural innovations. Certainly one fifteenth, possibly more, of the land of England changed its nominal ownership in this way within a very few years. Moreover, other confiscations of corporate lands followed in 1545 and 1547. The lands at both periods were seized and became temporarily possessions of the crown, only to be granted or sold, almost immediately, to courtiers or official speculators. The lands were for the most part whole manors, where the new owners became manorial landlords, with the usual group of rights. Others were simply certain amounts of land or houses, held as freehold by the old corporations in various manors and towns, and now coming into similar possession of the purchasers or grantees. The possibility of such extensive and complete transfers giving further impetus to undesirable changes could hardly escape the attention of Henry VIII and his ministers. In the first act of confiscation,

[1] Robert Crowley, *Epigrams*, lines 1169-1192, Early English Text Society ed., pp. 40, 41.

therefore, it was provided that new owners of monastery lands should reside on the estates thus acquired, and keep up the same amount of tillage as before.

" To kepe or cause to be kept an honest contynewell hous and houshold in the same scyte or precinct, and to occupye yerely asmoche of the same demeanes in plowyng and Tyllage of husbondry, that ys to saye asmoche of the seid demeanes which hath ben commonly usyd to be kept in Tyllage by the Governors, Abbotts or Pryours of the same Howses, Monasterys, or Pryoryes or by the fermer or fermers occupyeng the same wythin the tyme of twenty yeres next before this acte." [1]

The obverse of the same danger, that is the possibility of a more equitable and useful distribution of the lands, or of their application to more valuable public purposes than in the time of their old owners, was also recognized.   Starkey, in a letter to Henry VIII, probably in 1537, wrote as follows : " But here ys a thyng wych many wyse men feare and gretely dystrust, and what hyt ys I schal to your hyghnes brevely declare.   Hyt ys openly jugyd and commynly thought that the ferme and occupying of thes abbays and monasterys schalbe leysyd and set un-to grete lordys and gentylmen of much possessyonys and to them wych have therof no grete nede at al, the wych dowteles, yf hyt so be, schal much deface and gretly dymynysch the profyt of your acte and publyke utylyte, for then shall the grete commodyte therof run but to few and to such wych myght lake hyt ryght wel, and your pepul thereby schalbe lytyl then increasyd ; whereas yf the fermys therof were leysyd by copyhold, and of a mean rent, to yongur bretherne lyvyng in servyce unprofytabully and to them wych be of lowar state and degre, they schold gretely helpe to set forward chrystyan cyvylte and much increase the nombur of your pepul, specyally yf the ferme of the hole monasterys and demaynys of the same were dyvydyd in-to

[1] 27 Henry VIII, ch. 28, § 17.

sundry portyonys and dyverse holdys, and not leysyd to one to
turn hyt un-to a graunge.   And thys thyng schold not be
utturly wythout reson and gud consyderatyon, for pytye hyt
were that so much feyre howsyng and gudly byldyng, wych
myght wyth commodyte be maynteynyd to the comfort of man
schold be let fal to ruyne and dekay, whereby our cuntrey
myght appere so to be defacyd as hyt had byn lately overrun
wyth ennymys in tyme of warre, the wych must nedys ensew
yf the hole monastery be leysyd but to one to whome hyt
schal not be necessary to maynteyne so much housyng, but
a schyppe-cote peraventure schalbe to hym suffycyent." [1]
Another instance is to be found in one of Crowley's Epigrams.

> " As I walked alone,
>   and mused on thynges
> That have in my time
>   bene done by great Kings
> I bethought me of Abbayes,
>   that sometyme I sawe,
> Whiche are nowe suppressed
>   all by a lawe.
> O Lorde (thought I then)
>   what occasion was here,
> To provide for learninge
>   and make povertye chere?
> The landes and the jewels
>   that hereby were hadde,
> Would have found godly prechers
>   which might well have ladde
> The people aright
>   that nowe go astraye,
> And have fedde the pore,
>   that famishe everye daye." [2]

But the whole history of the seizure and disposition of the
monastery possessions is shameful.   Unworthy means were

---

[1] Printed in *England in the Reign of Henry VIII*, by the Early English Text
Society, p. lviii.

[2] *Epigrams*, lines 57–66, Early English Text Society ed., p. 7.

adopted to reach what was perhaps a justifiable end ; the
wealth of the monasteries was frittered away in the running
expenses of the government, or in extravagant gifts to unworthy
courtiers ; the debts of the crown were not completely paid,
no considerable permanent provision was made for religious,
educational, or charitable objects.   And as to the land changes
to which the government was so opposed, what the statute was
intended to ward off, and what Starkey feared, was exactly
what happened.

> " We have banyschyd superstysyon,
>   but styll we kepe ambysyon ;
> We have showtt awaye all cloystrers
>   but styll we kepe extorsynares ;
> We have taken there landes for ther abbwese,
>   but we have convertyd theme to a worse use." [1]

The lands were very generally obtained in large grants by
persons who were already landowners, and who were especially
addicted to absenteeism and inclosure.

The contemporary testimony as to the monasteries is, as we
should expect, where the individual cases must have differed
so much, and where the personal equation is so influential,
quite contradictory.   There can be little doubt that the abbeys
were, on the whole, conservative landowners and lenient landlords.   "They never raised any rent, or took any incomes or
garsomes [2] of their tenants, nor ever broke in or improved any
commons, although the most part and the greatest waste
grounds belonged to their possessions.   If any poor people
had made their moan at their day of marriage to any Abbey
they should have had money given to their great help.   And
thus all sorts of people were helped and succoured by abbeys ;
yea happy was that person that was tenant to an abbey, for it
was a rare thing to hear that any tenant was removed by taking

[1] *Vox populi, vox Dei*, 1547, Ballad Society Pub., vol. I, p. 139, lines 536–540.
[2] Fines.

his farm over his head, nor he was not afraid of any reëntry
for non-payment of rent, if necessity drove him thereunto.
And thus they fulfilled the works of charity in all the country
round about them, to the good example of all lay persons that
now have taken forth other lessons, that is, *nunc tempus alios
postulat mores.*" [1]   Again, Becon says of the successors of the
monks, "They abhor the names of monks, friars, canons, nuns,
&c.; but their goods they greedily gripe.   And yet where the
cloisters kept hospitality, let out their farms at a reasonable
price, nourished schools, brought up youth in good letters,
they do none of all these things." [2]

In a spirited dialogue, dated 1528, one of the disputants
says of the abbeys,

> " Their townes and villages
>   With out exaccions or pillages
>   Under theym have moche wynnynge." [8]

But his opponent contends,

> " Their townes somtyme of renowne
>   Leawdly they cause to faule downe
>   The honoure of the londe to marre.
>
> *   *   *   *   *
>
> Take hede howe farmers go backwarde
>   And thou shalt se it wyth thyne ey.
> For the londes welth pryncipally
>   Stondeth in exercyse of husbandry
>   By encreace of catell and tillynge.
> Which as longe as it doth prosper
>   The realme goeth backwarde never
>   In stabill felicite perseverynge.
> The abbeys then full of covetyse
>   Whom possessions coulde not suffyse
>   Ever more and more encroachynge.

---

[1] *The fall of religious houses*, Cole MSS. (British Museum), **XII**, fol. **5**,
quoted in Cunningham, *Eng. Industry and Commerce*, I, 473.

[2] Thomas Becon, *Jewel of Joy*, works, in Parker Society ed., p. 435.

[8] William Roy, *Rede me and be nott wrothe*, Arber Reprint, p. 97.

> After they had spoyled gentill men
> They undermyned husbande men
>   In this manner theym robbynge.
> Wheare a farme for 20£ was sett
> Under 30 they wold not it lett
>   Raysynge it up on so hye a some ;
> That many a goode husholder
> Constrayned to geve his farme over
>   To extreme beggary did come." [1]

But though the monasteries may have raised their rents in some places, and even, as More declares, inclosed their lands, it can hardly have been a frequent occurrence. The very decay of the monasteries, which had been in progress for at least a century, must have made them less likely to introduce changes. Their lack of enterprise, their failure any longer to attract men of parts in devotion, in intellect, or in business ability, had brought the greater number of the monasteries with all their lands into a condition of bankruptcy as real in material as in spiritual affairs. On the other hand, the courtiers of Henry VIII and the councilors of Edward VI, who received the bulk of the lands confiscated from the abbeys, were almost as generally inclosers as the merchants from the city who bought or leased landed estates. It was, indeed, just this process of obtaining lands and increasing their value that made possible the growth of the lower gentry and government officials of the early Tudor period into the new wealthy and cultured nobility of Elizabethan and later times. Innovators in religion, emancipated by their greater intelligence, their habits of travel, and their recent entrance into the aristocracy from the bonds of tradition and the habit of class responsibility, aliens to the locality where they became owners of the land, it is no wonder that the purchasers of the abbey lands were ready to introduce new methods, and became the most typical of inclosers, sheep farmers and rent raisers.

[1] William Roy, *Rede me and be nott wrothe*, Arber Reprint, p. 99.

"Qui auctores sunt tantae miseriae? Sunt illi, qui hodie passim in Anglia praedia monasteriorum pravissimis annuis redditibus auxerunt. Hinc omnium rerum exauctum pretium : hi homines expilant totam republicam. Villici et coloni universi laborant, parcunt, corrodunt, ut istis satisfaciant. Hinc tot familiae dissipatae, tot domus collapsae. Hinc quod omnium miserrimum est, nobile illud decus et robur Angliae, nomen, inquam, Yomanorum Anglorum fractum et collisum est. Nam vita, quae nunc vivitur a plurimis, non vita, sed miseria est." [1] So much the schoolmaster; but in plain English we find the same complaint. "Consyder you, what a wickednes is comonly used thorow the realme unponysshed, in the inordinate in-hansyng of rentys, and takyng of unresonable fynys, and every day worse than other ; and evyn of them specially to whom the kyng hath geven and sold the landys of those impys of anti-christ, abbays, and nonryes : which landys being in their handys, but only for that thei led us in a false fayth (as their com-panyons the byshops still doo) — but for the faythes sake, I say (for the which thei were justly suppressyd), it had bene more profytable, no dowte, for the comon welth, that thei had remayned styll in their handys. For why ? thei never inhansed their landys, nor toke so cruel fynes as doo our temporal tyrannys. For thei cannot be content to lete them at the old price, but rayse them up dayly, evyn to the cloudys, eyther in the rent or in the fyne, or else both ; so that the pore man that laboryth and toyleth upon it, and is hys slave, is not able to lyve." [2] And again, in a tract published the year before Henry's death, and protected in its plain speaking by being anonymous : "They buy at your Highnes hand such abbay landes as you appoint to be sold. And, when they stand ones

[1] Roger Ascham, *Letter to the Duke of Somerset*, Nov. 21, 1547, Giles' ed. *Ascham's Works*, vol. I, pp. 140, 141, quoted in Schanz's *Englische Handels-politik*, vol. I, 467.

[2] Henry Brinklow, *Complaynt of Roderyck Mors*, ab. 1542, Early English Text Society ed., p. 9.

ful reared therein, they make us youre pore commons, so in
dout of their threatynges, that we dare do none other but
bring into their courtes our copies taken of the coventes of the
late dissolved monastaries, and confirmed by youre Hygh
Court of Parliament, thei make us beleve that, by the vertue
of your Highnes sale, all our former writynges are voyde and
of none effect. . . .

" So that we your poore commons, which have no groundes,
nor are able to take any at these extorsioners handes, can fynd
no way to set our chyldren on worke, no, though we profer
them for meat and drynk and poore clothes to cover their
bodies. Helpe, merciful Prynce in this extremite; suffer not
the hope of so noble a realme utterly to perysh, through the
unsatiable desyre of the possessioners. Remember that you
shal not leave this kyngedome to a straunger, but to that child
of great towardness our most natural Prince Edward ; employ
your study to leave hym a Commune Weale to governe, and not
an iland of brute beastes, amongest whom the strongest devour
the weaker. . . .

" For the bloud of all them that through your negligence shal
perysh, shalbe required at your hand. Be merciful therefore
to your selfe, and us your most obeisant subjects. Indanger
not your solle by the sufferyng of us, your poore commons, to
be brought all to the names of beggers and most miserable
wreches. Let us be unto your Highnes, as the inferiour
membres of the body to their head. Remembre that your
hore heares are a token that nature maketh hast to absolve
the course of your lyfe." [1]

We have met more than once before with this mention of
the prevalence of pauperism in the period we are discussing.[2]
" For thys ys sure, that in no cuntrey of Chrystundome, for
the nombur of pepul, you schal fynd so many beggarys as be

---

[1] *A Supplication of the Poore Commons*, 1546, Early English Text Society
ed., p. 81.   [2] See pp. 26, 32, 40, 48.

here in Englond, and mo now then have byn before tyme."[1]
"Where as now London, beyng one of the flowers of the
worlde as touchinge worldlye riches, hath so manye, yea
innumerable of poore people forced to go from dore to dore,
and to syt openly in the stretes a beggynge, and many not able
to do for other, but lye in their howses in most grevous paynes,
and dye for lacke of ayde of the riche, to the greate shame of
the, oh London!"[2] Nor was this merely the impotent mass
of the halt, the maimed, the blind, the aged, which make up
the poor who are always with us. It included great numbers
of men, women, and children whose only reason for poverty
seemed to be their inability to find a place where their labor
could be made to fulfill their needs. The "sturdy beggar" was
at that time a comparatively new phenomenon. More's oft-
quoted argument,[3] it will be remembered, was called forth by
a supposititious conversation on this very point of the rapid
increase of pauperism. The number of wandering beggars,
vagabonds, or "strong thieves," for these classes shaded into one
another, became greater and greater through the whole of the
reigns of Henry VIII, Edward VI, Mary, and Elizabeth, until
the long series of attempts at solution of the problem reached
their culmination in the Poor Law of Elizabeth of 1601.[4]
Almost as late as that date Stubbes writes: "There is a certayne citie in Ailgna,[5] called Munidnol,[6] where as the poore lye
in the streetes, upon pallets of strawe, and wel if they have
that too, or els in the mire and dirt, as commonly it is seene,
having neither house to put in their heades, covering to keepe
them from the colde, nor yet to hyde their shame withall,
pennie to buy them sustenaunce, nor any thing els, but are

---

[1] Starkey, *Dialogue between Pole and Lupset*, Early English Text Society ed.
p. 89.

[2] Henry Brinklow, *Complaynt of Roderyck Mors*, Early English Text Society
ed., p. 90.

[3] *Utopia*, Arber Reprint, pp. 39–41.   [4] 43 Elizabeth, ch. 3.

[5] Anglia or England.   [6] Londinium or London.

suffered to dye in the streetes like dogges or beastes, without any mercy or compassion showed to them at all." [1]

This increase of homelessness and dire poverty was undoubtedly the result of several concurrent causes; but one cannot read of the evicted families of the peasant farmers, one cannot realize the new subjection of the lower classes to the stress of competition, without recognizing that pauperism was a natural, perhaps an unavoidable accompaniment of the whole series of changes which we have been engaged in tracing.

IX. In the almost universal condemnation of the whole series of rural changes, it is to be noticed that the principal elements of these changes were approved of and encouraged by two or three contemporary writers. Thomas Tusser, born in Essex in 1523, educated at Eton, "not without many stripes," as he tells us, and afterwards at Cambridge, lived many years as a sort of gentleman farmer in Suffolk and Norfolk, but later in life removed to London, and there published, in 1557, a curious book called "Five Hundred Points of Good Husbandry, as well for the Champion or open Country, as also for the Woodland or Several, mixed in every Moneth, with Houswifery, over and besides the Book of Houswifery." He devotes a whole chapter of verse, in which rhyme frequently predominates over reason, to pointing out the superiority of inclosed over uninclosed farming land:

> " The Countrey inclosed I praise,
> the tother delighteth not me.
> For nothing the wealth it doth raise
> to such as inferiour be,
> How both of them partly I know
> here somewhat I mind to shew.
>
> There [2] swine-herd that keepeth the hog,
> there neat-herd with cur and his horn,

---

[1] Stubbes, *Anatomie of Abuses*, reprint of 1836, p. 50, quoted in Ballad Society Pub., vol. I, p. 32.   [2] *I.e.*, in the uninclosed country.

There shepheard with whistle and dog,
    be fence to the meadow and corn.
There horse being ti'd to a balk,
    is ready with thieff for to walk.

Where all things in common do rest,
    corn-field with the pasture and mead,
Though common ye do as the rest,
    yet what doth it stand you in stead?
There commons as commoners use,
    for otherwise shalt thou not choose.

*   *   *   *   *

More plenty of Mutton and Beef,
    corn, butter and cheese of the best;
More wealth any where (to be brief)
    more people more handsome and prest,
Where find ye ; go search any coast,
    than there where inclosure is most:

*   *   *   *   *

What foot-paths are made and how broad,
    annoyance too much to be born,
With horse and with cattel what road
    is made through every mans corn:
Where champions ruleth the rost,
    there daily disorder is most.

Their sheep when they drive for to wash,
    how careless such sheep they do guide ;
The Farmer they leave in the lash
    with losses on every side.
Though any mans corn they do bite,
    they will not allow him a mite.

*   *   *   *   *

More profit is quieter found,
    where pastures in several be,
Of one silly Aker of ground,
    than champion maketh of three.
Again, what a joy is it known,
    when men may be bold with their own;

The tone is commended for grain,
    yet bread made of beans they do eat:
The tother for one loaf hath twain,
    of Mastline, of Rie, and of wheat.
The champion liveth full bare
    when woodland full merry do fare.

*   *   *   *   *

In woodland the poor men that have
    scarce fully two akers of land
More merrily live and do save,
    than tother with twenty in hand.
Yet pay they as much for the two
    as tother for twenty will do.

The labourer coming from thence,
    in woodland to work any where,
I warrant you, goeth not hence,
    to work any more again there.
If this same be true (as it is)
    why gather they nothing of this ;

The poor at inclosure do grutch,
    because of abuses that fall,
Lest some man should have but too much,
    and some again nothing at all.
If order might therein be found,
    what were to the several ground." [1]

But Tusser was probably not really contemplating the process of changing from champion to inclosure, of which he seems to have seen little. He was rather comparing those parts of the country where he found inclosures already made, his "woodland," with those which were still lying uninclosed. The superiority in the style of farming and in the wealth of the inclosed districts seems to have been generally acknowledged. The new farming was evidently superior to the old.

[1] Thomas Tusser, *Five Hundred Points*, *etc.*, chap. LII, ed. 1672, pp. 96–99.

As a matter of fact, there was a certain amount of inclosure for purposes of grain-farming, and in other cases sheep-farming may not have proved to be so lucrative as had been hoped, and therefore a return made to grain-farming under improved circumstances.   The Knight in the Dialogue says: " Experience should seme plainlie to prove that Inclosures should be profitable, and not hurtfull to the common weale; for we se that countries, wheare most Inclosures be, are most wealthie, as Essex, Kent, Devenshire, and such.   And I hard a civilian once saie, that it was taken for a maxime in his lawe, this sainge, that which is possessed of manie in common, is neglected of all; and experience sheweth that tenauntes in common be not so good husbandes, as when every man hath his part in severall." [1]   There is little question of the truth of this last remark.   The same opinion is expressed by another contemporary writer, of especial enlightenment.   Sir Anthony Fitzherbert, who wrote two well-known volumes, *The Book of Surveying and Improvements*, and *The Book of Housbandry*, declares in the latter, published in 1523, "and thoughe a man be but a farmer, and shall have his farm for twenty years, it is lesse cost for him and more profyt to quickeset, dyche, and hedge, than to have his cattell go before the herdesman." The chapter already alluded to in his other work, devoted to showing the greater income obtainable from an inclosed manor is as follows: " It is undoubted that to every townshyppe that standeth in tyllage in the playne countery there be errable landes to plowe and sowe, and leyse to tye or tedder their horses and mares upon, and common pasture to kepe and pasture their catell, bestes and shepe upon.   And also they have medowe grounde to gette their hey upon.   Then lette it be knowen howe many acres of errable landes every man hath in tyllage; and of the same acres in every felde to chaunge with his neyghbours, and to ley them toguyder, and

---

[1] W. S., *Discourse of the Common Weal*, 1549, Lamond's ed., p. 49.

to make hym one several close in every felde for his errable landes, and his leyse in every felde to lay them toguyeder in one felde, and to make one severall close for them all. And also another severall close for his porcyon of his common pasture, and also his porcyon of his medowe in a severall close by itself, and all kepte in severall both in wynter and somer and every cottage shall have his portion assigned him accordyng to his rent, and than shall not the ryche man overpresse the poore man with his catell and every man maye eate his owne close at his pleasure. . . . Now every husbande hath six severall closes whereof three be for corne, the fourth for his leyse, the fifth for his commen pastures, and the sixth for his hay; and in wynter time ther is but one occupied with corne and than hath the husbande other five to occupye till Lent come and then he hath his falowe felde, his ley felde, and his pasture felde, all somer. And whan he hath mowen his medowe than he hath medowe grounde." [1] But Fitzherbert is evidently picturing a change from the old form to the new through the general consent and participation of all the population on the manor, which was far from being the case in the actual development of inclosures. The possibility of such a voluntary rearrangement was, however, contemplated by others also. The Doctor in the Dialogue says: "for if land weare severallie inclosed, to the intent to continue husbandrie theron, and everie man, that had right to commen, had for his portion a pece of the same to him selfe Inclosed, I thincke no harme but rather good should come therof, yf everie man did agre theirto." [2] And even the husbandman says: "And everie day some of us encloseth a plote of his ground to pasture; and weare it not that oure grounde lieth in the common feildes, intermingled one with a nother, I thincke also our feildes had bene enclosed, of a common agreament of all the townshippe, longe ere this

---

[1] Sir Anthony Fitzherbert, *Book of Surveying and Improvements.*
[2] W. S., *Discourse of the Common Weal*, Lamond's ed., p. 49.

time." [1] Again : "But of late divers men, findinge greater profitte by grasinge then by husbandrie, have founde the meanes, either to by theire neighbors partes round about theim, or els to exchaunge with them so manie acres in this place for so manie in another; whearby they might bringe all theire landes together and so inclose it." [2]

But as a matter of fact, the inclosures and their accompanying changes did not usually occur in the voluntary way here alluded to, or contemplated by Fitzherbert. On the contrary, we have the dark series of pictures of the poor people turned out of their little holdings, and wandering away to swell the increasing mass of floating pauperism; another class retaining their cottages and farms, but paying a fine for renewal that absorbed all their savings of years previously, and subjected to a rent the payment of which kept those that clung to the old ways continually near starvation. Even the formal language of a government report gives glimpses of the weeping tenants leaving their old homes. The record in the Report of the Inquisition of 1517 states that the Prior of Wenlock converted thirty acres to pasture, "per quod duo aratra deponuntur et duodecim persone que ibidem occupari solebant ea occasione, a tenura et mansionibus suis *lamentabiliter* recesserunt." [3] And similarly of Puddleston in Herefordshire: "Item, Quod est messuagium decasum in Puddleston similiter et cotagium cum una virgata terre eidem messuagio adjacente in tenura domine Margerie Devereux nuper uxoris Johannis Devereux militis, et inhabitantes ejusdem pro defectu reparacionis predicta abinde *lacrimose* recesserunt." [4]

Whatever the advantages of the new organization over the old, the disruption of the latter involved so much that was

1 W. S., *Discourse of the Common Weal*, Lamond's ed., p. 56.

2 *Ibid.*, p. 124.

3 *Transactions of the Royal Historical Society*, 1892, p. 178, Leadam, editor.

4 *Ibid.*, 1893, p. 266.

sorrowful or that seemed injurious that barely these two or three contemporary writers have favored the change.

X. The increase of sheep-farming, inclosures, turning out of tenants, consolidation of farms, the rise of rents, were all closely and necessarily connected. It is to be noticed that many of the same disadvantageous results flowed from a different and quite independent cause. This was the increase of parks, sometimes merely as pleasure-grounds, sometimes as preserves for deer and rabbits. Harrison says : "In everie shire of England there is great plentie of parkes, whereof some here and there (to wit, welnere to the number of two hundred, for his daily provision of that flesh), apperteine to the prince, the rest to such of the nobilitie and gentlemen as have their lands and patrimonies lieng in or neere unto the same. I would gladlie have set downe the just number of these inclosures to be found in everie countie; but sith I cannot so doo, it shall suffice to saie, that in Kent and Essex onelie are to the number of an hundred (and twentie in the bishoprike of Durham), wherin great plenty of fallowdeere is cherished and kept. As for warrens of conies, I juge them almost innumerable. . . .

"In returning therefore unto our parks, I find also the circuit of these inclosures in like manner conteine oftentimes a walke of four or five miles, and sometimes more or lesse. Wherby it is to be seene what store of ground is emploied upon that vaine commoditie." [1]

The creation of these parks was in many cases a very recent matter. The higher gentry had been repeating on a smaller scale the old "afforesting" of the Norman and Angevin kings. Naturally some of the same evils reappeared.

"Oh Lord God, that it wold please the to open the earys of the kyng, lordys, and burgessys of the Parlament, that thei may heare the cryeng of the peple that is made thorow the reame for the inclosyng of parkys forestys and chasys, which

---

[1] *Description of England*, Bk. II, ch. 17, New Shakspeare Soc. ed., pp. 303, 304.

is no small burden to the comons.   How the corne and grasse
is destroyed by the dere many tymys, it is to pytyful to heare !
It is often sene, that men, joyning to the forestys and chasys,
have not repyd half that thei have sowne, and yet sometyme
altogether is destroyed.   And what land is your parkys ?   Be
not the most part of them the most batel and fruteful grownd
in England ? " [1]   Most of the complaints, however, are of the
same evils as were considered to flow from sheep-raising:
depopulation, evictions, diminution of food-supply.   "Where
in times past, manie large and wealthie occupiers were dwelling
within the compasse of some one parke, and thereby great
plentie of corne and cattell seene, and to be had among them,
beside a more copious procreation of humane issue, whereby
the realme was alwaies better furnished with able men to serve
the prince in his affaires; now there is almost nothing kept
but a sort of wild and savage beasts, cherished for pleasure
and delight; and yet some owners, still desirous to inlarge
those grounds, as either for the breed and feeding of cattell,
doo not let dailie to take in more, not sparing the verie
commons whereupon manie towneships now and then doo
live. . . .

"But if a man may presentlie give a ghesse at the univer-
salitie of this evill by contemplation of the circumstance, he
shall saie at the last, that the twentieth part of the realme is
imploied upon deere and conies alreadie, which seemeth verie
much if it be dulie considered of." [2]

The making of deer parks and extravagant building of
houses in them are frequently rebuked in the rising puri-
tanical spirit of the middle of the century.   As early as 1535
Lupset, in the Dialogue, declares: " Now you schel see many

---

[1] Henry Brinklow, *Complaynt of Roderyck Mors*, Early English Text Soc. ed.,
pp. 16, 17.

[2] Harrison, *Description of England*, Bk. II, ch. 17, New Shakspeare Soc. ed.,
pp. 306, 307.

men byld more then they themselfe, or theyr heyrys and suc-
cessorys, be convenyently abyl to maynteyn and repayre. And
so such housys as by some are byldyd to theyr grete costys
and charge, by other are let downe, and sufferyd to fal into
ruyne and dekey, bycause they were byldyd above theyr state,
condycyon, and degre." [1] In 1550 Crowley tells the Gentleman:

> " For parkes of dere thou shalt not care
> Neither for costuose buildyng." [2]

Some of the wealthier nobles made themselves especially
obnoxious by their extensive imparking. The Duke of Norfolk was one of the most conspicuous of these, the suits
between him and his tenants on account of rival claims to
certain commons extending to the government after his execution and the confiscation of his possessions. There is little
doubt that the downfall of Buckingham was made easier by his
local unpopularity, due to his inclosures for deer-parks. In
the report of 1517 there are three separate statements of
illegal inclosures by him: " Edwardus dux Bukingham 24 No-
vembris anno 24 Regis henrici VII apud Thornebury in comitatu
predicto de novo imparcavit in parcum suum ibidem vocatum
le newe parke 172 acras terre de dominicis terris suis propriis
et 96 acras terre et 32 pasture quas tenantes dicti ducis per
copias curie ad voluntatem dicti domini ducis occupaverunt de
hereditate dicti ducis.

" Et idem dux 10 die Januarii anno 6 Regis henrici VIII
elargavit parcum suum predictum vocatum newparke et ad
eundum apposuit et cum ffossis et palis inclusit 116 acras
terre de dominicis suis terris ibidem et 47 acras pasture quas
tenentes dicti ducis per copias curie ad voluntatem dicti ducis
occupaverunt de hereditate dicti ducis.

---

[1] Thomas Starkey, *Dialogue between Pole and Lupset*, Early English Text Soc.
ed., p. 96.

[2] *The Last Trumpet*, lines 1205, 1206, Early Eng. Text Soc. ed., p. 91.

" Et idem dux 10 die Januarii anno 6 Regis henrici VIII
elargavit parcum suum de Morlewood apud Thornebury predictum et ad eumdem apposuit et cum palis includi fecit 164
acras terre ibidem de dominicis terris suis propriis et 16½
acras pasture quas tenentes dicti ducis per copias curie ad
voluntatem dicti ducis præantea occupaverunt de hereditate
dicti ducis." [1]

The sixteenth century was a period of rapidly growing wealth
for certain classes. The favored gentry of the Tudor policy,
the officials who grew rich from salaries or peculations made
possible by the larger activities and expenditures of government, the town merchants who succeeded in foreign trade, the
country landowners who rose on the crest of the wave of agricultural change, were all amassing wealth in greater degree
than had been known in any but exceptional cases before.

> " For thay that of latt did supe
>   owtt of an aschyn cuppe,
>   are wonderfully sprowng upe :
>   That nowght was worth of latt,
>   Hath now a cubborde of platt,
>   his tabell furnyscheyd tooe
>   with platt be-sett I-nowe,
>   parsell gylte and sownde,
>   Well worth two hundred pound." [2]

In addition to this, country life had become more peaceful to
the upper classes than it had been before. Moats were no
longer dug around manor houses, because there was no longer
danger of violent attacks from hostile neighbors. Dwellings
could be built with a view to beauty and comfort rather than to
strength for defense. A more intellectual tone spread abroad
with the "new learning." Under these circumstances, — a
larger wealthy class, more security, more variety of ideas, — a

---

[1] Leadam's edition, *Transactions of the Royal Historical Society*, 1892, p. 188.
[2] *Vox populi, vox Dei*, lines 250–258. Ballad Soc. Pub., vol. I, p. 131.

real love for rural life spread throughout the upper classes; a habit which has imprinted its mark deeply on English sixteenth-century literature. The creation of parks and the "costuose building" were a natural result of this tendency. The latter gave us the Elizabethan country house; the former unfortunately seems to have involved many of the same deplorable results as did sheep-farming.

XI. The writers of the time, when they pass beyond mere denunciation, seem to have relied in the first place on moral influences, and secondly on these incentives reinforced by pressure from above, to reverse a movement which seemed to them entirely bad. Latimer says: "In thys realme are a great meany of folkes, and amongest many, I knowe but one of tender zeale, at the mocion of his poore tennauntes, hath let downe his landes to the olde rentes for their reliefe. For goddes love, let not him be a Phenix, let him not be alone, Let hym not be an Hermite closed in a wall, sum good man follow him and do as he geveth example." [1] In the *Book of Private Prayer*, set out by Edward VI in 1553, the following Prayer for Landlords was introduced:

"The earth is thine (O Lord), and all that is contained therein ; notwithstanding thou hast given the possession thereof unto the children of men, to pass over the time of their short pilgrimage in this vale of misery ; We heartily pray thee, to send thy holy Spirit into the hearts of them that possess the grounds, pastures, and dwelling places of the earth, that they, remembering themselves to be thy tenants, may not rack and stretch out the rents of their houses and lands, nor yet take unreasonable fines and incomes after the manner of covetous worldlings, but so let them out to other, that the inhabitants thereof may both be able to pay the rents, and also honestly to live, to nourish their families, and to relieve the poor: give

[1] *Fyrste Sermon of Mr. Latymer before Edward VI*, 1549, Arber Reprint, p. 42.

them grace also to consider, that they are but strangers and pilgrims in this world, having here no dwelling place, but seeking one to come: that they, remembering the short continuance of their life, may be content with that that is sufficient, and not join house to house, nor couple land to land, to the impovershment of other, but so behave themselves in letting out their tenements, lands, and pastures, that after this life they may be received into everlasting dwelling places: through Jesus Christ our Lord. Amen." [1]

Again, long afterwards, Stubbes says: "God give them grace to laye open their inclosures againe, to let fall their rents, fines, incommes, and other impositions wherby God is offended, the pore brethren beggered, and I feare mee, the whole realme will be brought to utter ruine and decay." [2]

Promises and threats based upon prospects in a future life were freely dispensed: "Wherefore if Inclosers and depopulaters of touns meane to be saved at the day of judgment, let them willingly cast open their closes againe and reedifie the farmes they have decaied. It makes no matter for the charge of hedging which they shall lose that they have been at. And let them banish their sheepe out of their pastures, and let them fill the Lords townes and sheepefolds with his sheepe again, and that speedily." [3]

> " Let the pore man have and enjoye
>   The house he had by copyehold,
> For hym, his wyfe, and Jacke hys boye,
>   To kepe them from hunger and colde ;
>   And thoughe the lease thereof be solde,
> Bye it agayne though it be dere,
> For nowe we go on oure laste yere:

---

[1] *The Primer; or Book of Private Prayer. Sundry Godly Prayers for Divers Purposes*, printed in *Liturgies of Edward VI*, Parker Society Publications, p. 458.

[2] Philip Stubbes, *The Anatomie of Abuses*, reprint of 1836, p. 126.

[3] Francis Trigge, *Humble Petition of Two Sisters ; the Church and Commonwealth*.

Caste downe the hedges and stronge mowndes,
   That you have caused to be made
Aboute the waste and tyllage groundes,
   Makeyng them wepe that erste were glad,
   Lest you yourselfes be strycken sadde,
When you shall se that Christe doeth drye
All teares from the oppressedis eye.

Restore the fynes, and eke the rent,
   That ye have tane more then your due ;
Else certenly you shall be shent,
   When Christe shall your evidence view ;
   For then you shall fynde these wordes trew,
You are but stuardes of the lande,
That he betoke into your handes." [1]

Others, however, seem to have looked to pressure from the temporal powers for an effective influence. More follows up his diatribe against inclosures by such a suggestion : " Make a lawe that theye whiche plucked downe fermes and townes of husbandrie shal reedifie them or els yelde and uprender the possession thereof to suche as wil go to the coste of buylding them anewe." [2] And we find repeated propositions that the government should require the lowering of rents to their former scale. For instance:

" Theis raginge Rentis muste bee loked uppon,
and brought unto tholde accustomed Rente,
as they weare let att fortie yearis agone :
then shalbe plentie and moste men content,
thoughe greate Possessioners liste not tassent :
Yeate, bettre it weare their Rentis to bringe undre,
then Thowsandis Thowsandis to perische for hungre.

[1] Robert Crowley, *Pleasure and Payne*, lines 470–490, Early English Text Society ed., pp. 122, 123.
[2] Sir Thomas More, *Utopia*, 1516, Robinson's translation, Arber Reprint, p. 43.

In whiche youre highnes this ordre maye take,
discreit men of youre counsell too assigne
that wilbee corrupted fo no mannys sake:
and theye withe helpe their endever tenclyne,
over youre Royalme wheare this is owte of lyne.
Groundis and ffermys to peruse and surveye:
Rentis to reforme that bee owte of the weye.

And as their Wisedomes (with Conscience) shall see
(the soyle consydered, barrayne or fertyle)
the Owners (by them) ordered to bee
their Rentis tabate, enhaunced so longe while." [1]

As a matter of fact, the government had taken action in regard to inclosures and some of their results long before the earliest of these appeals, and as was natural, in opposition to the whole movement. Notwithstanding its innovations in religion the whole policy of the Tudor dynasty was essentially conservative. Although the period was one of such radical change, the instinct of the rulers was to hold fast to the old ways, in proportion as they felt them slipping away from them. Moreover, the introduction of sheep-farming was considered, as we have seen, to involve a number of perfectly tangible evils which were especially distasteful to the administration. It threatened to deplete the country of its men, who were needed for soldiers, to raise the price of agricultural products, to spread sedition and readiness for rebellion, and to increase that army of wandering " sturdy beggars," which was being rapidly mobilized during the first half of the sixteenth century. It was but natural, then, that the government should endeavor to put a stop to changes so subversive of the old established order, and apparently so opposed to the interests of the state. The opposition lasted from the reign of Henry VII until the shrewdness of Elizabeth's ministers began to distinguish between the different elements of the movement,

[1] William Forrest, *Pleasaunt Poesye of Princelie Practise*, 1548, printed in *England in Henry VIII's Time*, Early English Text Society, p. xcvii.

opposing some and encouraging others, according to their estimate of their respective ultimate tendencies. But by this time the influences tending to rural change had about exhausted their force. It is one of the strongest forms of testimony to the strength of the social movement of that period that it could advance to its completion notwithstanding the steady opposition of the strong Tudor monarchy.

The first interposition of the government was by a law passed in 1488, applying only to the Isle of Wight, and intended to meet a special danger. Its preamble explains this : " For as moche as it is to the Kyng our Sovereign Lordis grete suertie, and also to the suertie of the Realme of England, that the Isle of Wight in the Countie of Southampton be wele inhabited with English people, for the defence as well of his auncien ennemyes of the realme of Fraunce as of other parties, the which Isle is late decayed of people by reason that many Townes and vilages been lete downe and the feldes dyked and made pastures for bestis and cattalles. And also many dwelling places, fermes, and fermeholds have of late tyme ben used to be taken in to oon mannys hold and handes, that of old tyme were wont to be in many severall persones holdes and handes and many severall householdes kepte in theym, and therby moche people multiplied, and the same Isle therby well inhabited, the whiche nowe by thoccacion aforseid is desolate and not inhabited, but occupied with bests and catall, so that if hasty remedy be not provided that Isle can not be longe kepte and defended, but open and redy to the handes of the Kingis ennemyes, which God forbeed." [1]

The law goes on to provide that no man should hold more farms on lease than one, if the total rent he pays exceeds ten marks a year. If any man in the Island already rents several farms, the total rent of which amounts to more than that sum, he must choose one or more of the farms which together fall within

[1] 4 Henry VII, ch. 16, Statutes of the Realm, II, 540.

it, and give up his leases of the others.   In the same year, a second statute was passed,[1] applying to the whole country, directed more especially against the transfer of land from tillage to pasture, and putting the burden upon the owners, not the renters of the land.   It was enacted that if a person owned any house or houses that had been connected with as much as twenty acres of land, where the land had been used at any time during the preceding three years in tillage or husbandry, he was bound to keep such houses in repair and the land in tillage, not allowing them to be diverted to any other use. Twenty-seven years afterward the matter came up again, under the government of Henry VIII.   In 1514 a petition was presented to the king, protesting especially against the engrossing of many small farms into the hands of one man.   A royal proclamation in enforcement of the existing law was drawn up, at least, if not issued, in the same year.[2]   At the Parliament held 1514–15, a law was passed which practically amounted to a reënactment of that of Henry VII, except that it required, in addition, that all houses and towns which had fallen into decay because of the substitution of pasture for tillage should be " reëdefyed and made ageyn mete and convenyent for people to dwele and inhabyte in the same, and to have use and therin to exercyse husbondry and tyllage."[3]   This act was only to continue until Christmas of the same year, but·in the next year it was reënacted in permanent form.[4]   In 1517, a Royal Commission was appointed to investigate inclosures and report such as had been made since the first year of Henry VII, that is, during the preceding thirty-four years.   A thorough inquiry was made, and a report sent in to the government.   A great

[1] 4 Henry VII, ch. 19, Statutes of the Realm, II, 542.
[2] This Petition and Proclamation are printed in the Ballad Society Publications, vol. I, pp. 101–103.
[3] 6 Henry VIII, ch. 5, Statutes of the Realm, III, 127.
[4] 7 Henry VIII, ch. 1, Statutes of the Realm, III, 176, 177.

part of this report still exists, and has been recently published.[1] It gives much insight into the nature of the inclosures, but does not seem to have been followed by any immediate legislation or other action on the part of the government.

A possible result of the Inquisition of 1517 is, however, to be found in the fact that on the 12th of July, 1518, Cardinal Wolsey, as Lord Chancellor, issued a decree in Chancery that all who had pleaded the king's pardon or submitted to his mercy for inclosures should within forty days "pull down and lay abroad" all inclosures and ditches made since the first year of the reign of Henry VII, under a penalty of £100, unless they could bring evidence that such inclosure was more beneficial to the commonwealth than the pulling down of it would be, or that it was not against the statutes about the decay of houses.[2] Then the matter slept, as far as the government was concerned, for some fifteen years, when in 1534 it was brought up again in the "Reformation Parliament." The earlier acts of Henry VII and Henry VIII were formally renewed, the prohibition of taking more than one farm on lease was changed so that no man should take more than two, and the second of these only in the case of its being in the parish in which he already lived. But the main provision of this law was an attempt to go farther back in its action than earlier statutes by restricting the number of sheep which any one man could own. This maximum number was placed at 2000, by the long hundred, that is, 2400 by actual count. This restriction was modified considerably, however, by the concession that landowners, both clerical and lay, could keep any number of sheep they wanted on their own demesne lands and pastures. The application of this limitation would therefore be only to those who occupied

[1] *Transactions of the Royal Historical Society*, 1892, 1893, and 1894. Edited by J. S. Leadam, Esq.

[2] *Calendar of Letters and Papers*, Rolls Series, Henry VIII, vol. II, pt. ii, p. 1546.

leased or copyhold lands.   It was indeed these against whom
the statute was directed, as the words of the preamble indi-
cate: "how they myght accumulate and gather together into
few hands as well great multitude of fermes as greate plentie of
catall and in especiall shepe, puttyng suche lands as they can
gett to pasture and not to tyllage, wherby they have not only
pulled downe churches and townes, and inhansed the old ratis
of the rentis of the possessions of this Realme . . . by reason
wherof a mervaylous multitude and nombre of the people of
this Realme be not able to provyde meate, drynke, and clothes
necessary for theymselfes, theire wifes and childern, but be so
discoraged with myserye and povertie that they fall dayly to
thefte, robberye, and other inconvenience or pitifully dye for
hunger and colde; And as it is thought by the kynges most
humble and lovyng subjects that one of the gretest occasions
that moveth and provoketh those gredy and covetous people
so to accumulate and kepe in theire handes suche great por-
cions and parties of the groundes and landis of this Realme
from the occupying of the poure husbondmen, and so to use it
in pasture and not in tyllage, is only the greate profette that
commyth of shepe which now be commyn to a few persons
handes of this Realme in respecte of the holle nomber of the
Kynges Subjectes, that some have twenty four thousand, some
twenty thousand, some ten thousand, some six thousand, some
five thousand, and some more and some lesse." [1]   In all the
acts in which the return of land to tillage and the rebuilding
of houses was provided for, the penalty for violation was the
confiscation of one half the income by the next superior feudal
lord until the law was complied with.   In 1535, an act was
passed complaining that in cases where lands were held directly
from the king the law was obeyed, but where held from lesser
lords, it was not.[2]   It was therefore ordered that the king

[1] 25 Henry VIII, ch. 13, Preamble, Statutes of the Realm, III, 451–454.
[2] 27 Henry VIII, ch. 22, Statutes of the Realm, III, 553, 554.

could have in twelve of the counties of England one half the
income from all lands and houses where the law was uncom-
plied with. By 1535, Henry VIII was becoming used to
obtaining income from confiscations. There is still but little
indication of the law having any effect. In 1549, Latimer
says, "we have good statutes made for the commen welth as
touching comeners, enclosers, many metinges and sessions,
but in the end of the matter their commeth nothing forth." [1]
In the previous year, however, 1548, the Protector had initi-
ated a new movement against the inclosures. In the hope of
calming the agitation of the people, he issued on the first of
June, 1548, a proclamation [2] calling attention to the laws
already on the statute-book, announcing the appointment of
a new Commission on Inclosures, and commanding all who
knew of offenses against the law to give information of the
same to the king's Commissioners. The same day a commission was issued for at least one circuit, including the counties
of Oxford, Berks, Warwick, Leicester, Bedford, Bucks, and
Northampton. [3] The instructions given by the king to the
Commissioners include nineteen points, requiring a report of all
instances of depopulation on account of the introduction of
pasture-farming, and of the creation of parks, of violations of
the laws restricting the number of sheep in one person's hands
to 2000, making two farms the maximum number which one
tenant could hold, and requiring the keeping up of tillage on
lands confiscated from the monasteries. [4]

On one circuit only, the one already referred to, and of
which John Hales, apparently the instigator of this whole
effort, was a commissioner, is there any evidence of activity.
In the central counties of England they made a strenuous

[1] *First Sermon before Edward VI*, Arber Reprint, p. 41.
[2] Printed in *Discourse of the Common Weal*, Lamond's ed., pp. 148–150.
[3] Strype, *Ecclesiastical Memorials*, II, ii, 348–351.
[4] *Ibid.*, pp. 359–361. Printed in fuller form by Grafton in 1549.

effort to obtain complete information of violations of the law. They met every kind of opposition. The great landowners and inclosers overawed the poorer classes to prevent their giving information, or arranged to have their own servants placed on the local juries to give perjured testimony. The spirit of the law was found to have been violated in various ingenious ways. Where houses of husbandry were required to be kept up, owners had taken away the lands for pasture, but allowed some shepherd or milkmaid to live in the house ; to conform to the law requiring the lands to be retained in tillage, they had plowed and planted a single furrow about a large tract of land, feeding their sheep on the remainder ; and in order not to possess more than the statutory 2000 sheep, they held them in the name of children, kinsfolk, or servants.[1] In addition to local difficulties, protests were continually made by members of the King's Council like Paget, Warwick, and others who disapproved of the objects of the Commission. In the autumn session of Parliament, in the same year, Hales brought in three bills intended to meet the difficulties in the enforcement of earlier statutes against inclosures. The first of these was apparently on the old lines, the second directed against the buying and immediate selling of cattle, the third requiring that for every hundred sheep above the first one hundred and twenty that any man kept in several pasture, he should keep two cows and rear one calf. The first and last of these bills failed of passage, the second was passed in a modified form only.[2] There is no doubt that the opposition of Parliament, especially of the gentry who were represented in the House of Commons, was interested; and such legislation against inclosures as was carried was in response to the pressure of the executive and of public opinion, not in accordance with

[1] See *Hales' Charge*, Strype, *Ecclesiastical Memorials*, II, ii, 362.
[2] See *Hales' Defense*, written from Coventry, September 1, 1549, printed in Lamond's edition of the *Discourse of the Common Weal*, pp. lii–lxvii.

the wishes of the landowning members of Parliament. The Commission resumed its work in the next year, but, becoming more or less involved in the rising tide of disorder of the summer of 1549, accomplished nothing further. No general report by them is known to exist. In 1552, however, a new statute was passed,[1] defining the time of application to the period since the first year of the reign of Henry VIII, and providing a method of enforcement by which commissioners should be appointed from time to time to ascertain through the country, by sworn juries, how much land had been cultivated in each manor for any four consecutive years, and to compel the continued cultivation of an equal amount, under penalty of five shillings per acre for every year in which such land remained in pasture. In November of the same year, the King's Council issued a proclamation to the justices of the peace, charging them with the execution of this statute : but this was much like setting the cat to watch the cream ; the magistrates were the principal beneficiaries of the inclosures ; no commissioners were appointed, and there is no evidence of a more effective enforcement of this than of former statutes. In Mary's second year an " Acte for the Reëdification of decayed Houses of Husbandrie and for the increase of Tyllage "[2] was passed, specifically reënacting the law of Henry VII, continuing the provision for the occasional appointment of commissioners, and authorizing the destruction of recently enclosed rabbit warrens.

Early in Elizabeth's reign, in July, 1561, Cecil sent letters to all the magistrates in the southern and western counties, bidding them send in reports on the working of various laws affecting the daily life of the people, including the laws against turning tillage to pasture.[3] The reports of the magistrates, if

---

[1] 5 Edward VI, ch. 5.   [2] 2 and 3 Philip and Mary, ch. 2.
[3] *Domestic MSS.*, Elizabeth, vol. XX, quoted in Froude, *History of England*, VII, 473, etc.

made, are not known to exist, but a possible result is to be found in the reënactment, in the next year, of the laws of Henry VII and Henry VIII against inclosures.   This statute [1] also repealed the laws of Edward and Mary on the subject, as being partially imperfect, partially too mild.   No new principle was added to the law, except that the penalty for allowing land formerly tilled to remain as pasture was increased to ten shillings per acre, per year.   There was no new legislation or other action of the government in the matter for thirty years. It seems then to have been considered either that the movement of inclosures was over, or that they were beneficial rather than injurious, for the law of 1562 was deliberately repealed, thus removing from the statute book almost all legislation against the agricultural changes.[2]   This was a condition of freedom that had not existed legally for more than a hundred years, during which period inclosures, and the conversion of old tillage land to pasture, must have been made in the great majority of cases in violation of the law.   And the landowners and large tenants seem to have taken advantage of their opportunity.   Five years afterward, the government was forced to reënact laws against inclosures, acknowledging the increased rapidity of the decay of villages, and impressed most strongly, apparently, by the resulting increase of vagabondage.[3]   One half of all farmhouses decayed more than seven years before the act were to be rebuilt, and all of those intentionally allowed to fall during the seven years immediately preceding the act.   A suitable amount of land was to be attached to each house, for tillage purposes.

In the same year a still more stringent law was passed, on the same lines,[4] but applying only to the central counties of England, and only to land converted to pasture since the

---

[1] 5 Elizabeth, ch. 2.   [2] 35 Elizabeth, ch. 7.
[3] 39 Elizabeth, ch. 1.   [4] 39 Elizabeth, ch. 2.

beginning of Elizabeth's reign. Four years later these statutes were still further extended.[1]

When James I came to the throne the later laws of Elizabeth on this subject were reënacted, among a large number of others, probably quite as a matter of form.[2] The matter was, however, brought again quite suddenly from the realm of formality to that of reality, by the series of riots that swept over Northamptonshire and Warwickshire in the early spring of 1607. A proclamation against these rioters was issued on May 30, and another on June 28. The Council took the matter of enclosures into immediate consideration. It seems to have been at this Council meeting of July 5 that a carefully drawn up paper, which is still preserved, was presented by some one of the members.[3] This paper, after questioning the propriety of reforms during a period of disorder and violence, proceeds to lay down the belief that inclosures are in the main desirable, that conversion from tillage to pasture is good wherever the occupier finds it profitable ; and that the real harm is to be found only in the engrossing of several farms into one man's hands, and in any resulting depopulation. This was a reversion to the very earliest law on the subject, and acknowledged the propriety of much that was at the time unlawful. It proposed, therefore, a repeal of all the old laws, and the enactment of a new one, providing that no lord of a manor should hold more than one quarter of its extent as demesne, that the remaining three quarters should be divided into farms, none of which should exceed one hundred acres, and that no man should hold more than one of these. This plan seems to have been adopted as the policy of the administration, for a proclamation announcing the intentions of the government was issued four days afterward, and a pardon for the rioters on the twenty-

[1] 43 Elizabeth, ch. 9.   [2] 1 James I, ch. 25.
[3] Printed in Cunningham's *Growth of English Industry and Commerce*, II, pp. 701–703.

fourth of the same month.   A commission of inquiry was then
sent through the disturbed districts.   The report of the
commissioners is in the Record office, but it has never been
published.   A second proclamation of pardon to the rioters,
issued March 30, 1608, seems to have closed the matter.   The
proposed statute was not passed and the question dropped out
of consideration with the cessation of the disorders.[1]

Twenty years afterward Parliament passed a general law
repealing many obsolete or disapproved statutes, and among
these are included the laws against inclosures of Henry VII,
Henry VIII, and Edward VI, and that of the fifth year of
Elizabeth.[2]   This left still in force the laws of Elizabeth's last
years, but it acted probably as a general repealing statute.
The economic development of the nation relieved the government from further necessity of considering inclosures and the
increase of pasture-farming as a general movement.   The laws
had been, with one short interval, consistently antagonistic to
one of the strongest economic movements of the time.   But
the instruments through which the Tudor monarchy habitually
acted, the lesser nobility, the country gentry, and the official
class were opposed to their enforcement, so that their influence, appreciable as it must have been, was comparatively
ineffective.

XII.   It might well be supposed that changes so generally
condemned, as we have seen them to be, by observers who had
no direct connection with the movement, and so frequently
legislated against by the government, would arouse still more
active opposition, and even resistance, from those who suffered
under them.   The annals of the mass of the people are not
written by themselves.   The record of their feelings has come
down to us only in chance fragments.

[1] State Papers, Domestic, James I, quoted in Gardiner, *History of England*, I,
p. 355.
[2] 21 James I, ch. 28.

" Lay out, lay out,[1]
Hore Law and Hollinghey Clough ! "

was the refrain that the ghost of some early incloser was
supposed to utter as it wandered through the park of
Townley, in Lancashire, a park which had formerly been
village common land.   The people who still occasionally saw
the spirit and heard its words of remorse, had apparently
forgotten its earthly name until a later local historian dis-
covered a government grant of " all that parcel of land called
Hore Law pasture, containing by estimation 194 acres of 24
feet to every perch, abutting on the north upon a pasture
called Hollinghey, parcel of the possessions of the Duchy
of Lancaster, and formerly inclosed in severalty by John
Townley, Knight." [2]

Leland also records that " Edward, Duke of Buckingham,
made a fayre Parke hard by the Castle, and tooke much faire
grownd in it very frutefull of corne, now fayr Launds, for
coursyng. .The Inhabytaunts cursyd the Duke for ther
Lands so inclosyd.   There was also afore Duke Edward's tyme
a Parke at Estewood a myle or more of, but Duke Edward at
two tymes enlargyd it to the Compase of six myles, not without
many Cursys of the poore Tenaunts." [3]   But at certain times
the opposition did not stop at mere " cursys."   A paper of this
period, though of uncertain date, gives an indication of the
rising tide of desperation.

" The Diggers of Warwickshire to all other Diggers.

" Loving Freinds and subjects, all under one renowned Prince,
for whom we pray longe to continue in his most Royall estate,
to the subverting of all those subjects, of what degree soever,

---

[1] *I.e.*, remove the inclosing hedges from.
[2] Letters-Patent, Feb. 28, 1603; in Whitaker's *Whalley*, vol. II, p, 188.
[3] John Leland, *Itinerary*, Hearne's translation, vol. VII, fol. 75 a.

that have or would deprive his most true harted Commonalty both from life and lyvinge. Wee, as members of the whole, doo feele the smart of these incroaching Tirants, which would grinde our flesh upon the whetstone of poverty, and make our loyall hearts to faint with breathing, so that they may dwell by themselves in the midst of theyr Hearde of fatt weathers. It is not unknowne unto your selves the why these mercyless men doe resist with force against our good intents. It is not for the good of our most gracious Soveraigne, whom we pray God that longe he may reygne amongst us; neyther for the benefitt of the Commonalty, but onely for theyr owne private gaine; for there is none of them but doe tast the sweetness of our wantes. They have depopulated and overthrown whole Townes, and made thereof sheep pastures nothing profitable for our Commonwealth. For the common Fields being layd open would yeeld us much commodity, besides the increase of corne, on which standes our life. But if it should please God to withdrawe his blessing in not prospering the fruites of the Earth but one yeare (which God forbidd) there would a worse and more fearfull dearth happen than did in King Edward the seconds tyme, when people were forced to eat Catts and Doggs flesh, and women to eate theyr owne children. Much more wee could give you to understand but wee are perswaded that you your selves feele a part of our greivuances, and therefore need not open the matter any plainer. But if you happen to shew your force and might against us, wee for our partes neither respect life nor lyvinge; for better it were in such case wee manfully dye, then hereafter to be pined to death for want of that which these devouring Encroachers doe serve theyr fatt Hogges and Sheep withall. For God hath bestowed upon us most bountifull and innumerable blessings, and the cheifest is our most gracious and Religious Kinge, who doth and will glory in the flourishing estate of his Commonalty. And soe wee leave you commending you to the sure hold and

safeguard of the mighty Jehova, both now and evermore.
From Hampton field in hast:

> Wee rest as poore Delvers and Day labourers for the
> good of the Commonwealth till death.
>
> A. B. C. D. &c." [1]

Again, their feelings are stated in a pamphlet of 1546:
" These men cesse not to oppresse us, your Highnes pore
commons, in such sort that many thousands of us, which here
before lyved honestly upon our sore labour and travayl,
bryngyng up our chyldren in the exercise of honest labore, are
now constrayned some to begge, some to borowe, and some to
robbe and steele, to get food for us and our poore wives and
chyldren. And that whych is most lyke to growe to inconvenience, we are constrained to suffer our chyldren to spend
the flour of theyr youth in idlenes, bryngyng them up other
to bear wallettes, other eles, if thei be sturdy, to stuffe prisons,
and garnysh galow trees." [2]

The Pilgrimage of Grace in 1536, although ostensibly and
principally made on religious grounds, received much of its
impetus from the misery of the people, due to inclosures. It
was utilized by the nobles and the priests for their own purposes, but the mass of the people who marched with Aske and
d'Arcy had originally risen in rebellion in the hope of putting
an end to inclosures and evictions. Among the demands of
the rebels prepared to be presented at the second meeting at
Doncaster, the thirteenth section is: " The statute for inclosures and intacks to be put in execution, and all inclosures and
intacks since 4 Henry VII, to be pulled down, except moun-
tains, forests, and parks." But as the religious changes
became more generally accepted by the people the social

---

[1] *Harl. Ms.* 487, leaf 9, printed in Ballad Socie*y Publications, vol. I, p. 37.

[2] *Supplication of the Poore Commons*, in *Four Supplications*, published by the
Early English Text Society, p. 79.

changes emerged as the great remaining object of discontent. The possibility of a rebellion of the peasantry was already recognized.

> " Yf yow doo not redresse
> betymes this covitisness
> My hede I wold togage
> ther welbe grett owtrage
> Suche rage as never was sene
> in any olde manes tyme." [1]

Finally, in the early part of 1549, the resistance came to a crisis. A wave of rioting passed over the southern and western counties, then further eastward and northward through most of the midlands, till it reached its culmination in " Kett's Rebellion " in Norfolk. The people tore down the hedges and palings of the parks, filled up the ditches, and laid open again the common pastures and arable lands which had been inclosed. Various causes contributed to bring about the rising, but that inclosures and the hatred of the common people for the inclosing gentry were the most efficient we have contemporary testimony. " The causes and pretences of thes upprores an Risynges are diveres and uncerteine, and so full of varietye almost in Every Campe, as they call them, that it is hard to write what it is; as ye knowe is lyke to be of people without head and Rulle, And that wold have that they wotte not what, some Criethe 'plucke downe inclosures and parkes'; some for their Comones; otheres pretende the Relygeone; A number wold Rulle an other whille and directe things as the gentlemene have done; And indeed, all hath Convayed a wonderfull hate agaynste gentlemen, and takethe them all as their Ennemyes." [2]

A contemporary historian puts the following speech into the mouths of the rebels : —

---

[1] Ballad, *Vox populi, vox Dei*, lines 767–771, 1547 or 1548, Ballad Soc. Pub., vol. I.

[2] *Letter from Duke of Somerset*, Cotton MS., Galba, B. xii, leaf 115. Printed in Ballad Soc. Pub., vol. I.

"The commons which were left by our forefathers for the reliefe of ourselves and families are taken from us, the lands which were within the remembrance of our fathers open are now surrounded by hedges and ditches, and the pastures are enclosed, so that no one can go upon them. We will throw down hedges, fill up ditches, lay open the commons, and level to the ground whatever enclosures they have put up."[1] The contemporary chroniclers give the same explanation. "A third sort of these mutineers were certain poor men that sought to have their commons again, by force and power taken from them ; and that a regulation might be made according to law of arable lands turned into pasture.[2] Hollinshed, referring to the Protector's two proclamations, the first announcing a Commission to oppose inclosures, the second against unlawful assemblies and rioting, says, " For wheras there were few that obeied the commandement, the unadvised people, presuming upon their proclamation, thinking that they should be borne out by them that had set it foorth, rashlie without order tooke upon them to redresse the matter ; and assembling themselves in unlawful wise, chose to them captains and leaders, brake open the inclosures, cast downe ditches, killed up the deare which they found in parkes, spoiled and made havocke, after the maner of an open rebellion."[3] Among the grievances and claims of the Norfolk rebels a goodly number are the familiar complaints of the yeomen of the time.

"We pray your grace, that no lord of no manner shall comon uppon the Comons.

"We pray that prestes frome hensforth shall purchase no londes, neyther ffre nor Bond ; and the londes that they have in possession may be letten to temporall men, as they wer in the ffyrst yere of the reign of kyng henry the VIIth.

---

[1] Neville, *De Furoribus Norfolcensium*, quoted in Scrutton, *Commons and Common Fields*, p. 88.   [2] Strype, *Ecclesiastical Memorials.*
[3] Hollinshed, *Chronicle*, III, 1002.

"We pray that Rede-ground and medowe grounde may be at suche price as they were in the first yere of kyng henry the VIIth. . . .

"We pray that all ffreeholders and copieholders may take the profightes of all comons, and ther to comon, and the lordes not to comon nor take profightes of the same. . . .

"We pray that copiehould londes that is onresonable rented, may go as it dyd in the ffirst yere of kyng henry the VII ; and that at the deth of a tenante, or of a sale, the same landes to be charged with an esey ffyne, as a capon, or a resonable some of money, ffor a remembrance. . . .

"We pray that it be not lawfull to the lordes of eny manner to purchase londes frely, and to lett them out ageyn by copie of court roll, to ther gret advauncement, and to the undoyng of your pore subjectes. . . .

"We pray that no lorde, knyght, esquyer, nor gentleman, do grase nor fede any bullockes or shepe, if he may spend fforty poundes a yere by his landes, but only for the provicion of his howse."[1]

Again, in 1552, there was an insurrection, this time quite local, in Buckinghamshire, but openly directed against the high rents lately introduced.

Rebellion, as usual, brought about not success but reaction. The popular risings were all put down with great severity. Northumberland, the successor of Somerset, was himself an extensive incloser, and disapproved of any limitation of the movement. Yet contemporary writers continued to attribute the excesses of the people to the oppression of the landlords. Within a year after the Norfolk rebellion, Crowley declared, "If I shulde demaunde of the poore man of the contrey what thinge he thinketh to be the cause of sedition, I know his answere. He woulde tel me that the great fermares, the

[1] Petition of Kett and the Norfolk Rebels, 1549, *Harl. MSS.*, 304, leaf 75. Printed in Ballad Society Publications, vol. I, p. 147.

grasiers, the riche buchares, the men of lawe, the marchauntes, the gentlemen, the knightes, the lordes, and I can not tel who ; men that have no name because they are doares in al thinges that ani gaine hangeth upon.   Men without conscience.   Men utterly voide of Goddes feare.   Yea, men that live as thoughe there were no God at all !   Men that would have all in their own handes ; men that would leave nothyng for others ; men that would be alone on the earth ; men that bee never satisfied. Cormerauntes, gredye gulles ; yea, men that would eate up menne, women, and chyldren, are the causes of Sedition ! They take our houses over our headdes, they bye our growndes out of our handes, they reyse our rentes, they leavie great, yea unreasonable fines, they enclose oure commens !   No custome, no lawe or statute can kepe them from oppressyng us in such sorte, that we know not whyche waye to turne us to lyve. Very nede therefore constrayneth us to stand agaynst them ! In the countrey we can not tarye, but we must be their slaves and laboure tyll our hertes brast, and then they must have al. . . .

"Better it were therefore, for us to dye lyke men, then after so great misery in youth to dye more miserably in age !" [1]

Another preacher, a few years later, brings the same indict-ment against the inclosers, adding to it a diatribe against the much disliked new nobility and gentry.

"I have heard it reported, that divers gentlemen have been the occasion of all these tumults and seditions, through the great oppressions and wrongs that they have done to the poor commons, as by making common pastures several to themselves, by inclosing more ground to their own use than heretofore hath been accustomed, and by this means take away the necessary food for the poor men's cattle, without the which they cannot live ; again, by getting so many farms into their hands, and letting out their own lands unto the tenants and

---

[1] Robert Crowley, *Waie to Wealth*, Early English Text Society, p. 133.

farmers for so great price, or else take such large fines and great incomes that they can never live of it. . . .

"Then is there another sort which glory in the title of gentleman also, and they are such as this common proverb noteth :

> As riseth my good,
> So riseth my blood.

They think all nobility to consist in the abundance of worldly goodes, in wearing of golden chains and costly apparel, in having fair houses and pleasant gardens. And to set forth this their gentlemanry, they poll, they pill, they wake, they rake, they sweat, they fret, they gripe, they nip, they face, they brase, they semble, they dissemble ; yea, they move every stone, as they say, to maintain and set forth their unnoble nobility, not caring how they come by it, so they have it. All is fish that cometh to the net : it is good to be taking. *Bonus est odor lucri ex re qualibet* [Juvenal, xiv. 204]. These study not, as the true gentlemen do, to profit many, to do good to the country, to maintain the poor, to relieve the succourless, to nourish the weak, to cherish their needy tenants; neither seek they the commodity of the commonweal, but their own private advantage. They labour to possess much, but they distribute nothing. Their hand is stretched out to receive, but shut when they should give. If they once creep into a town or village, they for the most part never cease, till they have devoured and eaten up the whole town. Whatsoever is pleasant or profitable must be theirs, by hook or by crook ; it lieth handsomely for them, and so near their nose, though it be a mile off. If there be either farm or sheep-ground, upon the which some honest poor man liveth, both he and his family, out he must. Had it must be, whatsoever it cost, though the poor man and all his should go a-begging, it lieth so commodiously for our new-come gentleman. If they buy any tenement, and let it out again to the poor man, O how do they rack it and stretch out the rents thereof, almost from a penny to a pound ! Yea, and some of them, buying house and land in a town, suffer the houses to fall down, and turn the ground unto pasture, the poor man not having where to hide his head." [1]

Through the reigns of Mary and Elizabeth there is no record of any actual insurrection attributable to the land changes. But much local disorder existed; the numerous rebellions for dynastic or religious objects found their ready material in the discontent of the people ; and the mass of pauperism, vaga-bondage, and crime was constantly reinforced by the progress of the same social changes. Early in the reign of James I, there seems, as we have seen, to have been a recrudescence of enclosures, which gave rise to a series of riots in Northamp-tonshire and Warwickshire so serious as to call for the inter-vention of the government. But a proclamation, an investi-gation, and a general pardon were sufficient without the use of troops. This was, in fact, an isolated outbreak. As in the comparatively rare mention of inclosures as late as the close of the sixteenth century or the beginning of the seven-teenth, the evidence leads to a belief that the movement was, for the time at least, practically over. During the last half-century circumstances had changed vastly. Population had been growing through the whole reign of Elizabeth; English manufactures were being developed, and commerce extended. All of this involved the raising of more food and therefore the greater profit in general farming. More liberal laws in regard to the exportation of grain tended also to a higher price and a more steady demand for agricultural products. Again, the coinage had been reformed, and the steady increase of currency through the products of the American mines acted as an impetus to the general economic development of the country.

[1] Thomas Becon, *Fortress of the Faithful*, Parker Society Publications, pp. 598,599.

A more satisfactory equilibrium in economic production, as in other directions, seems to have been attained, and distress and disorder subsided correspondingly. In the great mass of Elizabethan and Jacobean literature there is far less mention of social discontent than in the scanty pages of the prose and verse of the time of Henry VIII and Edward VI. What seems almost the dominant note of the writings of the first three quarters of the century is scarcely to be distinguished as any important constituent of the literature of the later period. Yet some elements of the movement we have been tracing still appear quite frequently. The rent-raising landlord is a familiar character in the later. drama, and long afterward, in a ballad of about 1635, a beggar boy sings:

> " My fields lie open as the highway :
> I wrong not the country by greedy inclosing."[1]

Or again, in a fine description of a model knight, it is said that " He raiseth no rent, racketh no lands, taketh no incombs, imposeth no mercilesse fines, envies not another, buyeth no house over his neighbour's head, but respecteth his country, and the commodity thereof, as deere as his life."[2]

In the year 1614 the town of Stratford was agitated by a proposition to inclose some of its open fields, and it is recorded in the diary of the town clerk that " Mr. Shakspeare told Mr. J. Greene that I was not abble to beare the enclosing of Welcombe,"[3] the open high land from which one looks down upon Stratford. Still, the inclosures had run their course for the time. The process was now a casual incident of local improvement, making little impression on general social history until the new influences and new conditions of another

---

[1] Roxburgh Collection, I, 543.

[2] Robert Greene, *Quip for an Upstart Courtier*, 1592, Collier's Reprint, p. 49.

[3] Town Records of Stratford, Sept., 1614, quoted in Halliwell-Phillipps' *Outlines of the Life of Shakspeare*, pp. 167–169.

age, after a century and a half of intermission, completed the work of the time we have been studying.

It cannot now be difficult to reconcile some of the apparent contradictions of the period of transition from the Middle Ages to modern times in England, to see how an age of advancing wealth, enterprise, and prosperity for certain parts of society should be a period of poverty, loss, and misery for others; to recognize that the entrance of a higher type of intellectual interest and of religious faith might be simultaneous with grave social evils and lower moral standards; to understand how a strong centralized monarchy, whose principal justification for existence was the preservation of order, was yet not strong enough to prevent changes which to most thoughtful men of the time seemed to threaten social chaos. The condition of affairs we have seen to be this: Mediaeval society, at least in its lower strata, was based on the idea of custom, — of status. Custom was embodied and perpetuated in small and local social bodies. The individual existed primarily as a member of some group, a village community, a town corporation, a gild, a monastic house. But the slow changes of a century or more had destroyed the equilibrium of this state of society. By the beginning of the sixteenth century two great influences were gaining strength: on the one hand, a feeling of individual independence and initiative, and, on the other, a new conception of national unity and national corporate existence. Both of these were destructive to the old local custom-bound life. If the individual was to free himself from the bonds which restrained him, he must sacrifice for himself, although at the same time he destroyed for others, the supports which upheld him and them. Again, if the nation was to be a reality to each person who composed it, the government must reach each individual directly. Therefore the smaller bodies to which men belonged were destined to sink into insignificance, no longer either absorbing the enterprise and independence of the individual, or supplanting the national state. The principal difference to the individual man was that he now had opportunity for independent action guaranteed to him by the state, whereas of old he had a customary status preserved for him by his manor court, his town, his gild, his religious order.

And in these new conditions there were many who suffered as surely as there were those who advanced. Some throve under enlarged opportunities, but others sank under the new competition and new risks. While some profited by the exemption from restrictive rules and by freedom to initiate new enterprises, many others fell into poverty and misery, from their incapacity to adapt themselves to new conditions. There are few things less mobile than human habits and human institutions, and this rigidness becomes greater as we go lower in society and backward into ruder conditions. The sixteenth-century farmers who had to leave the little holdings their ancestors had occupied for centuries were a characteristic, though by no means a solitary instance of a generation sacrificed to its own incompetence for change in the presence of a social movement which was practically irresistible.

The great accompanying changes of the time in religion, in government, in literature, in education, do not lie within the subject of this essay. It is true, however, that inclosures and sheep-farming, the transfer of capital from the towns to the country, the depopulation of hundreds of small hamlets, and the growth of a new farming class tell the same story of a new era as they do. Although when looked at from one point of view these are technical changes in agriculture and land-holding, in another and a broader aspect they are lines of least resistance in which certain forces acted, and thus give testimony to the existence of these new forces in society. The differences between historic periods, and the suddenness of passage from one to another may easily be exaggerated. Yet it is unquestionably true that there are long periods in which change is slow, and the pressure for change, although real and constantly accumulating, is inconspicuous.   Then follows a period in which these latent forces become almost suddenly operative, and changes are rapid and far-reaching.   In many aspects of society, preëminently in those homely phases which have been here described, the period of English history lying between 1475 and 1575 was such a time of rapid change, and therefore of especial significance.

BIBLIOGRAPHY.

Arranged approximately in chronological order.

ab. 1459. JOHN ROSS. A Warwickshire Antiquary. Died 1491. Edited by Thomas Hearne, 1745.

1480. Speech of Lord Chancellor, prepared for the opening of Parliament. Printed in two forms in Grants of Edward V, Camden Soc.

ab. 1486. Letter from the Vicar of Quinton to the Master of Magdalen College, Oxford. Printed as an Appendix to Denton's England in the Fifteenth Century.

1489. Statutes, 4 Henry VII, chs. 16, 19, Statutes of the Realm.

1514. Petition to the King, and Royal Proclamation. Printed in Ballads from MSS., Ballad Soc., vol. I.

1514–15. Statute, 6 Henry VIII, ch. 5, Statutes of the Realm.

1515–16. Statute, 7 Henry VIII, ch. 1, Statutes of the Realm.

1516. SIR THOMAS MORE. Utopia. Original edition, Louvain, 1516. Numerous editions and translations, and reprinted in Arber's Series.

1517. Report of Royal Inquisition into Inclosures. Printed in Transactions of Royal Historical Society for 1892, 1893, 1894. Edited by J. S. Leadam.

1518. Decree of Lord Chancellor. Calendar of Letters and Papers, Henry VIII, vol. II, pt. ii, Rolls Series.

ab. 1520. Ballad, Nowe-a-Dayes. Printed in Ballads from MSS., Ballad Society, vol. I.

1523. SIR ANTHONY FITZHERBERT. Book of Husbandry. Reprinted in the English Dialect Society Publications. Book of Surveying and Improvement. Reprinted in "Ancient Tracts on Husbandry."

1523. WILLIAM TYNDALE. Doctrinal Treatises, Parker Society Publications.

ab. 1527. WILLIAM ROY. Rede me and be nott Wrothe. Arber Reprint.

1534. Statute, 25 Henry VIII, ch. 13, Statutes of the Realm.

1536. Statute, 27 Henry VIII, ch. 22, Statutes of the Realm.

ab. 1536. THOMAS STARKEY. Dialogue between Pole and Lupset. Published by the Early English Text Society in a volume called England in the Reign of Henry VIII, in 1878, ed. by S. J. Herrtage.

1540. THOMAS BECON. Jewel of Joy, and Fortress of the Faithful. Parker Society Publications.

ab. 1540. Three Pamphlets, ed. by R. Pauli, or Drei volkswirthschaftliche Denkschriften aus der Zeit Heinrichs VIII.

1541. HENRY BRINKLOW. Complaynt of Roderyck Mors. Early English Text Society.

1546. Supplication of the Poor Commons. Printed in Four Supplications, Early English Text Society.

1547. ROGER ASCHAM. Works, Giles Edition.

ab. 1547. Ballad, Vox Populi, Vox Dei. Printed in Ballads from MSS., Ballad Society, vol. I.

Certayne Causes gathered together, showyng the Decaye of England by the Great Multitude of Sheepe. Printed in Four Supplications, Early English Text Society.

1548. Proclamation of the Protector Somerset against Inclosures.

Draft of a Bill against Inclosures.

Defense of John Hales.

These are printed in Lamond's edition of the Discourse of the Common Weal of this Realm of England.

Commission for Redress of Inclosures.

Charge of John Hales, one of the Commissioners.

Royal Instructions to Commissioners.

These are printed in Strype's Ecclesiastical Memorials, II, pt. ii; but the contemporary list of instructions printed by Grafton, 1549, is more full.

1548. WILLIAM FORREST. Pleasaunt Poesye of Princelie Practise. Extracts printed in England in Henry VIII's
Time. Early English Text Society.

1548–49. Latimer's Sermons before Edward VI. Arber Reprint.

1549. W. S. A Discourse of the Common Weal of this Realm
of England. Various editions; by far the best is that
by the late Miss Lamond, 1893.
Petition of Robert Ket and others. Printed in Ballad
Society Publications, Ballads from MSS., vol. I.

1550. THOMAS LEVER. Sermons. Arber Reprint.
ROBERT CROWLEY. Works, ed. by Cowper. Early Eng-
lish Text Society.
SIR JOHN COKE. Debate of the Heralds.

1552. Statute, 5 Edward VI, ch. 5, Statutes of the Realm.

1553. BERNARD GILPIN. Sermon before Edward VI. Printed
in Strype's Ecclesiastical Memorials, II, pt. ii.
Primer or Book of Private Prayers issued by Edward VI.
Parker Society Publications.

1555. Statute, 2 and 3 Philip and Mary, ch. 2, Statutes of the
Realm.

1563. Statute, 5 Elizabeth, ch. 2, Statutes of the Realm.

1573. THOMAS TUSSER. Five Hundred Points of Good Husbandry. Various editions; that of 1672 used here.

1577. WILLIAM HARRISON. Description of England. Prefixed
to Hollinshed's Chronicles of England. Reprinted by
New Shakspeare Society.

1583. PHILIP STUBBES. Anatomie of Abuses. Reprinted by
New Shakspeare Society.

1584. THOMAS LUPTON. Dream of the Devil and Dives.
JOHN LELAND. Itinerary of England, translated and
edited by Thomas Hearne.

1589. FRANCIS TRIGGE. A Defense of These Our Days.
Godly and Dutiful Sermon at Grantham, 1592.
Humble Petition of Two Sisters, the Church and the
Commonwealth, 1604.

1593. Statute, 35 Elizabeth, ch. 7, Statutes of the Realm.

1597.   Statute, 39 Elizabeth, chs. 1, 2, Statutes of the Realm.

1598.   THOMAS BASTARD.   Chrestoleros.   Seven Bookes of Epi-
           grames.

        Petition of Diggers of Warwickshire.   Printed in Ballads
           from MSS., Ballad Society Publications, vol. I.

1601.   Statute, 43 Elizabeth, ch. 9, Statutes of the Realm.

1603.   Statute, 1 James I, ch. 25, Statutes of the Realm.

1624.   Statute, 21 James I, ch. 28, Statutes of the Realm.

An almost complete list of sources for this subject is given in
Miss Frances Gardiner Davenport's "Classified List of Printed
Original Materials for English Manorial and Agrarian History during
the Middle Ages," Radcliffe College Monographs, No. 6.

The same subject is discussed in the following works:

W. J. ASHLEY.   English Economic History, vol. II.

WM. CUNNINGHAM.   Growth of English Industry and Commerce,
           vols. I, II.

J. E. THOROLD ROGERS.   History of Agriculture and Prices, vol. IV.

T. E. SCRUTTON.   Commons and Common Fields.

GEORG SCHANZ.   Englische Handelspolitik, vols. I, II.

W. OCHENKOWSKI.   Englands Wirthschaftliche Entwickelung im Aus-
           gange des Mittelalters.

ERWIN NASSE.   The Agricultural Land Community of the Middle
           Ages and the Inclosures of the Sixteenth Century.

In Froude's History of England there is much incidental mention
of the social movements of the time here referred to.

INDEX.

Open Fields, 8.
Owen, 45.

Parks, 4, 77.
Pasture, 13, 31.
Pauperism, 69.
Piers Plowman, 9, 11.
Population, 37, 41.
Primer, 82.

Quinton, 4.

Rebellion, 96, 98, 100, 103.
Rents, 45, 68, 83, 104.
Rogers, 24.
Ross, 4, 29.
Roy, 45, 65.

Scattered Acres, 9.
Shakspeare, 9, 30, 58.
Sheep-farming, 21, 84.
Small Farms, 12.
Somerset, 89, 99.

Starkey, 2, 34, 51, 59, 64, 70, 79.
Statutes, 12, 30, 34, 40, 54, 63, 70,
    85, 86, 88, 91, 92, 94.
Strype, 53, 89, 99.
Stubbes, 6, 31, 47, 70, 71, 82.
Supplication of Commons, 69, 97.

Tenants, 15.
Tenure, 13, 15.
Tillage, 37, 86, 93.
Townsmen, 54, 58.
Trigge, 2, 7, 8, 28, 34, 38, 82.
Tusser, 28, 71.
Tyndale, 48.

Vagabondage, 26, 32, 70.
Vox Populi, Vox Dei, 28, 50, 56,
    65, 80, 98.

W. S., 1, 2, 10, 22, 34, 41, 50, 56,
    74, 75, 89.
Wool, 23, 25.

Yeomen, 13, 33, 68.